Joe Pavelka

It's

Not About Time!

Rediscovering Leisure in a Changing World

Books that inspire, help and heal

Published by Creative Bound Inc.
P.O. Box 424, Carp, Ontario
Canada K0A 1L0
(613) 831-3641
www.creativebound.com

ISBN 0-921165-69-2
Printed and bound in Canada

Editor: Janet Shorten
Book design: Wendelina O'Keefe
Cover image © Digital Stock Corporation

Printing number 10 9 8 7 6 5 4 3 2 1

Canadian Cataloguing in Publication Data

Pavelka, Joseph Paul, 1964-
        It's not about time! : rediscovering leisure in a changing
world

Includes bibliographical references.
ISBN 0-921165-69-2

        1. Leisure. I. Title.

GV14.P39 2000   790'.01'35   C00-901248-6

For those who matter most…

Mary, Kailen Rose and Chloe Rae

I love you thi-i-i-i-s much!

Acknowledgments

I would like to acknowledge my long-time colleague Ann Dalhberg. Ann's editorial skill, patience and perseverance added clarity and confidence to this effort. Many thanks go out to Gail Baird, Janet Shorten, Barb Clarke and all the staff at Creative Bound for your support and for having faith in your intuition. I would also like to acknowledge Kenn Knights, Michael Kenny and Mumtaz Dhanidina for their support and for showing me how to see the forest for the trees. At the risk of repetition I have to thank my wife Mary for her support, patience and sacrifice (and even for her critical reviews) during the writing process. My dreams simply don't happen without you, Mary.

Contents

Introduction

For the past 15 years or so I have worked in various capacities in the leisure, recreation and tourism areas. In both my personal and professional life I have become aware of a growing frustration with the search for leisure experiences. People have so little free time, and what they do have is often not particularly satisfying in terms of finding leisure. Even traditional leisure activities are increasingly unreliable at providing a satisfying leisure experience, despite continued efforts by the leisure industry to understand the elusive nature of their product and please their clients.

But it is increasingly apparent that in spite of our standard of living, supposed free time and immense choice in the marketplace, we may be too stressed to enjoy ourselves. More importantly, my research into the definition of leisure and my efforts to understand the essence of the leisure experience have led me to believe that we may be looking for leisure in all the wrong places. Many of us are trying to find a deeply personal leisure experience outside of ourselves—through activities, free time and consumerism. The elusive nature of leisure may stem from a failure to appreciate its real essence. I believe that leisure is not primarily about time. Rather it is about the way in which we experience any moment, and about finding experiences that bring about self-expression and a strong connection with the world around us.

My research revealed that I was not the first to believe that leisure is actually a deeply personal state of mind brought about by experience. I have borrowed from the work of a variety of scholars; their influence is evident in the first section of the book, which is devoted to rediscovering a new and meaningful definition of leisure for today's changing world. As I began to rediscover different ideas of leisure as self-expression through my research, teaching, consulting and personal life, I discussed these ideas with anyone who would listen. With each discussion and workshop I witnessed more and more of an "aha" reaction as I shared my ideas and observations. These ideas resonated with people of all backgrounds and lifestyles because they too were eager to rediscover a meaningful and satisfying leisure life.

In this book, we will rediscover leisure—that essential ingredient in our quality of life that has always been there but may be hidden under that stack of papers on the desk. Section One concerns itself with a full exploration of leisure and our ability to experience it. In Chapter 2, I discuss the traditional definitions and associations that we have with leisure: leisure and free time, non-work, idleness, balance and recreation. Chapter 3 explores the essential elements of our new and more meaningful definition of leisure, and Chapter 4 introduces the concept of "leisure ability"—our ability to experience leisure given a host of internal and external motivators and barriers.

In Section Two, I turn to an examination of several larger social trends—related to economy, employment, crime, education, technology and government—that impact our ability to experience leisure. Events in the world around us influence our thoughts, attitudes and actions and this is also true of the leisure experience. We may not be able to change events and trends, but we can be aware of them and aware of how they affect us. In doing so, we become better equipped to negotiate our way through the world in the way that we choose, not simply in the directions we are pulled. In some cases, these trends will present us with opportunities to gain a richer leisure experience. In other cases they present obstacles to be negotiated.

The trends discussed in Section Two should resonate with both Americans and Canadians, as information sources come from both countries. Canadians and Americans are more alike than we are different; however, our priorities are not always the same. We both struggle with issues of time stress, social and moral turbulence, technology, globalization, crime and the economy. However, according to a *Maclean's* 1999 poll of 1,200 Canadians and 1,000 Americans, we do differ slightly in ranking our most important issues. For instance, Americans rank social and moral issues first; crime and violence second; and the economy, jobs and inflation third. Canadians rank social services, health and education as first; unemployment and economy second; and taxes third. Government spending and debt ranks fourth for both countries. Canadians rank crime and violence sixth, which is lower than Americans. Pollution and the environment are ranked sixth by Americans and seventh by Canadians. Finally, north of the border, national unity is ranked fifth, but this is not an important issue for Americans. These differences may be relevant to interpreting some of the trends discussed in Section Two.

Rediscovery is as much about the future as it is about the present, and in Section Three I examine our future prospects for leisure and discuss how we can transform the insights and information from the previous chapters into action that can change our lives. The stress created by the scarcity mentality perception that "the pie is shrinking," along with our predisposition to productivity over creativity, will directly influence our ability to experience leisure. The final chapter addresses some strategies to overcome these and other challenges on our way to rediscovering leisure in a changing world.

The Chapter References at the end of each chapter provide references to books and articles of particular significance for that chapter; at the end of the book, under "Related Reading," you will find titles of books and articles that explore further the subjects of leisure, time and quality of life.

It's Not About Time! will challenge, enlighten and empower. It has been kept brief, because the ultimate message is thankfully simple, and there is no need for reading it to become another source of time stress! This book will challenge us to rethink leisure, but in simple practical terms that are meaningful in everyday life. It will enlighten us on the myriad of everyday factors that impact our ability to experience leisure. Finally, it will empower us to negotiate our own leisure path, both now and in the future.

• Section One •

The Leisure Myth

• Chapter 1 •

Important and Elusive

In the 1960s, experts predicted that North Americans were headed for a leisure time boom like nothing we had ever seen before. At the start of the 1980s, we were supposed to be entering a leisure explosion, and by the early 21st century we were supposed to be working only three or four days a week. We were to have seen rapid and sustained economic growth with huge gains in wages, high levels of consumer confidence and very stable jobs. Technology was supposed to bring us into an era of household time-saving gadgetry, leaving us with little to do around the house except enjoy ourselves. The end result of these changes was to have been a lot of free time—so much free time that the challenge was going to be learning what to do with it.

What happened? For the answer we need to look back at the basis for these predictions, and the climate in which they were made. The major drivers behind the anticipated leisure boom were economics and technology, and they simply did not do what they were expected to do. From the 1940s to the 1960s real wages had skyrocketed along with economic growth in North America and there was very low unemployment and inflation. Economic indicators led to the conclusion that work and maintenance were going to be less of a drain on our daily time and energy. Assuming that these trends would continue well into the 1990s and beyond, simple mathematics dictated that the leisure "piece of the pie" would increase as the other pieces decreased.

But the assumption of continued wage increases was shattered in the 1970s, and there has been no upward spike since then. Economic forecasts did not materialize and therefore the assumption that work would be less of an everyday concern was not borne out. In fact, in the 1970s inflation added to financial worries, making work an even bigger part of everyday stress.

Meanwhile technology, which showed such great promise in the 1960s as the answer to the drudgery of housework, simply has not produced the expected results around the house. We have never come close to the ideals portrayed by George Jetson and his space-age family. The dishwasher, washer/dryer, microwave, household intercom and, later on, the personal computer and the cellular telephone have made us more efficient (at home and at work), but efficiency on its own has not given us more free time. It appears that we have misconstrued the purpose of these technological innovations as an opportunity to do more work with our time rather than reallocating the time to leisure.

What Our Lives Are Really Like

Here we are at the start of the new millennium and very few of us are worried about how to use our free time. For most of us, it has been so long since we had any that we cannot even remember what free time feels like. It is not that we are living in particularly difficult times—quite the contrary. As a population, we are doing very well. North Americans have a standard of living that is the envy of the world. But maintaining and improving on that standard of living is taking more and more effort. Some days, doing well feels likes it's killing us.

What happened to the leisure predictions of the 1960s? How did we change from a society anticipating excess leisure-time problems to one of the most time-stressed populations in the world?

A lot of things have changed in the decades since those predictions were made. For instance, we moved from the apparently endless booming economy of the '40s and '50s—when the predictions were made—to a much shorter-cycle boom-and-bust economy that has dramatically changed the way we think about money, work and security. The space age technology that was supposed to reduce or even eliminate household labor and thus give us free time has failed to do so. Time and labor-saving devices simply provided us with new opportunities to do more work, to take on more obligations. Modern concerns about safety and security require that children must be constantly supervised, and their lives require managing, structuring, schedule juggling and chauffeuring in a way that the previous generation could not have imagined.

If you are among the majority of adults in North America you have probably spent a few confused moments in the past year wondering just how you got to be so busy. You have probably endured many panic-ridden moments grappling with all the jobs on your day's to-do list, and in the middle of all that stress—if you could find another spare minute—you may have wondered whatever happened to leisure and leisure time.

The Importance of Leisure

Does it matter that we have so little leisure in our lives? Is leisure important? When asked this question, most people respond that leisure is a very important part of daily life—especially those who face the realities of time stress. Single mothers, working mothers, indeed almost all those between 25 and 55 who work for a living, are likely to say that leisure is a very important part of their lives, because compared to the rest of the population, they are the ones who most feel they have lost leisure.

The importance of leisure has been argued for centuries, dating back to the time of ancient Greece. That the debate continues today is proof of leisure's enduring importance. One area where we witness the growing importance of leisure is in the results of opinion surveys. A 1997 survey reported that over half of all Canadians think leisure is as important as work, if not more important. As more and more of us find that leisure is being squeezed out by our struggles with issues of day-to-day balance, time stress and other pressures, the importance of leisure appears to be growing.

The value of leisure is seen at cash registers as well. The amount of our disposable income dedicated to leisure products, services and travel is steadily increasing. Virtually all leisure industries have experienced steady and above-average growth, as demonstrated by the increasing numbers of new leisure services and products in the marketplace. Increasing growth of the leisure industry is expected, as the baby boomers move beyond the most time-stressed decades of their lives, and find themselves with both the time and the money for leisure. The industry is just beginning to take advantage of this new market. Within our aging society, leisure means big business.

Even software and Internet companies understand the enormous power of leisure as a way to introduce people to new technologies. New technologies are often introduced first in the form of leisure or play activities, and move on to more serious uses once they have become familiar and accepted. People warm to new technology best through play, as was found with the introduction of Nintendo and computer games. Virtual reality technology has several very serious medical and other potential applications, but it is making its way into the marketplace first through play.

The health care industry has also come on board, proclaiming the importance of leisure. Leisure participation is recognized as a way to improve health and fitness, thereby reducing health care costs. Likewise it is seen as a way to curb the psychological and social ills arising from stress. High-powered companies now promote leisure opportunities for their employees in an effort to improve health and therefore performance. Many community agencies such as police and social services use leisure as an effective way to achieve their goals in the community. Midnight basketball leagues in New York City use a recreational/leisure activity as a way to respond to the serious problem of youth crime and drugs. Providing new opportunities and directing the energy of young people into positive activity has proven very successful, and midnight leagues are now established in other major cities.

Most of us know at an intuitive level that leisure is essential to a positive quality of life, and its mental, social and physical benefits are obvious. We know that our peace of mind and well-being deteriorate when we are denied access to our favorite leisure activities for an extended period of time. Leisure, recreation and entertainment opportunities are clearly recognized as important criteria in rating the best places to live. The availability of leisure opportunities and participation in leisure are considered to be measures of a progressive society.

Less obvious, but no less important, is recognizing that leisure is our most genuine outlet for self-expression—our leisure is a reflection of who we really are. This point may be at the core of leisure's undisputed importance to each of us. In a world that often seems dominated by obligations, leisure is one area where we are able to put ourselves first. Whether at home, on a golf course or even at work, our leisure can be a direct reflection of how we see ourselves. We often have no choice about our "must-do" time and activities. We do these things because we *have to*. But in our free time, we do what we want to do, and what we choose to do reflects our true self. We can learn the most about a person—about their self-image, style and priorities—by looking at what they do in their unobligated time. Seeing how a person spends the time that they control tells a great deal about who they are, and how they see themselves. Whether we spend our free time gardening, participating in an amateur paleontology society, rock climbing or volunteering at a women's shelter, this activity is usually a direct clue to who we are and what we value, and is a direct and important form of self-expression. What makes leisure so important—especially in our present world, dominated by obligations and time commitments—is that leisure is something *we* can direct.

Generally speaking, then, leisure is important because it is essential to our quality of life and self-expression. And it is rendered all the more valuable, all the more important, by the fact that it is apparently becoming more and more scarce.

Have We Always Valued Leisure? A Love–Hate History

Although we recognize that leisure is an important aspect of our lives, it is also clear that our society approaches leisure with some ambivalence. Almost no one would deny its importance, whether from a quality of life or economic point of view. At the same time, our society clearly applauds one form of addiction: workaholism. So while we know in our hearts that our leisure lives are critical, we are rarely rewarded for pursuing leisure, but constantly rewarded for hard work and ambition. Our current ambivalent feelings toward leisure are not new—throughout history Western society has had a kind of love-hate attitude toward leisure. At different points in history, leisure has been revered as something to be cherished, and suppressed as a root cause of evil. Leisure has been an important way for any society to express its values, aspirations and fears, and this still holds true today.

For most of human history, there was no real distinction between leisure and its most obvious counterpart: work. With the development of agriculture in the last 10,000 years, there emerged a class structure, with segments of the population no longer directly involved in food procurement. One result was the establishment of at least one class of people who did not need to work for a living, and hence we have the origins of leisure as the opposite of work.

The ancient Greeks and Romans embraced an idea of leisure that was based on a philosophy of both self and community improvement. Leisure broadly meant striving to be a better person, and through sport, the arts and knowledge, the Greeks pursued the ideal of the complete man: an accomplished philosopher, statesman, merchant and warrior. While the Roman era entrenched the idea of a leisured class comprising people whose wealth and position meant they did not have to work to live, the Romans were also the first to make leisure opportunities accessible to everyone—even those of poorer classes. Public stadiums, baths and gardens were built for everyone to use. By the end of the Roman era, leisure had reached a peak of popular acceptance that was to crash along with the Empire.

The Dark Ages and the Early Christian era saw the pendulum swing toward a devaluation of leisure. Leisure was a casualty in the backlash against the decadence and open-mindedness of the Roman era, as stadiums, baths and public gardens were destroyed. Christianity emerged as the focal point around which society was organized, bringing with it notions of the here and the hereafter that resulted in a philosophy of strict self-denial and religious obedience. Sport, education, arts and free time activities were strictly forbidden for both adults and children, even though many of these leisure pursuits were practiced away from the authorities.

During the Renaissance, social authority shifted to the state and a broader idea of leisure became popular. Leisure was associated with self-expression through recreation, education and the arts. A host of free-time activities including pub-going and gambling were once again permitted. With the onset of the Protestant Reformation, however, leisure ideals and activities were again forbidden, continuing through the Calvinist period of the New World. Self-denial, strict religious values and economic production—that is, anything related to work—became important and valued. Anything even closely related to leisure, recreation or idleness was forbidden, as "the devil makes work for idle hands," and idleness was even outlawed in early Virginia. This was the period of the Protestant work ethic, a legacy that arguably remains with us today.

In the mid-1900s, following the end of World War II, North American society experienced unprecedented growth in virtually every area. Economic, population and technological growth were enormous, and with it leisure was again transformed into an accepted and legitimate part of everyday life. The economic conditions of the 1950s led to the leisure boom prediction discussed earlier. Leisure has become a legitimate part of our society, gaining respectability as an important ingredient in quality of life. Despite our deeply entrenched work ethic and tendency to prize hard work above all else, we clearly value a kind of leisure-like self-expression—whether it is pursued through family, work, education or health.

What Is Leisure?

Most of us think of leisure in terms of the traditional distinction between work and leisure, equating it with free time or some activity that we would pursue in our spare time. To the question "what is leisure?" typical answers would include free time, any time not at work, anything I choose to do in my free time, traveling, hobbies, play, entertainment, recreation, arts, sports, idleness or doing nothing. Indeed, leisure is so elusive and difficult to define in part because we have so many different ideas about what leisure really is. While most of us would agree that leisure is essential to our emotional and mental health and our overall quality of life, we are unlikely to agree on a definition of this most elusive of experiences.

Academics were among the first to offer a formal definition that reflected and solidified the notion of leisure as time. One of the leaders in the field of Leisure Studies, and one of the first to offer a definition, was Stanley Parker of Great Britain. He concluded that leisure was basically *any time not spent at paid work*. As academics gave more attention to the concept, it became clear that this definition was insufficient in that it lacked a recognition of our daily maintenance activities that were neither paid work nor leisure, activities that existed somewhere between work and free time. The addition of the maintenance category resulted in a broader definition of leisure, as *the time remaining after one's work and subsistence responsibilities are addressed*. This definition established these all-important time-based categories of work, maintenance and leisure, which remain a popular top-of-mind way of thinking of leisure today.

Is free time always leisure, and do leisure activities always provide a true leisure experience? That the answer to both questions is "no" highlights the difficulty in defining—and experiencing—leisure.

Clearly not all free time will count as leisure if we assume leisure to be a positive experience. Someone who is involuntarily unemployed and experiencing limited financial resources is unlikely to regard the long empty days as leisure. Likewise, a two-hour layover at an airport certainly counts as free time, but few of us would regard it as leisure. What is it about free time that makes it leisure?

In order for free time to be leisure, it has to be the right kind of free time. Tim the Toolman will not find an evening at the opera to be a satisfying leisure experience, any more than Jill, his wife, would enjoy an afternoon working on a car. So the time must be spent in appropriate activity. But the essence of this condition is self-image—in order to be an enjoyable experience, it has to support your self-image. A woman who sees herself exclusively or even primarily as a high-powered corporate executive or scientist is unlikely to find an hour in a playground, watching children play and visiting with their mothers, to be a valuable leisure experience. That same woman might well find such an hour to be a highly enjoyable leisure experience if her image of herself includes being a "mom among moms," and if she is free to enjoy it without worrying about a multitude of other tasks.

Let me give an example from my own life. I have always wanted to see myself as the father in an active outdoor family. I get great pleasure from images of myself and my wife and daughters skiing and hiking and taking canoe trips together. These experiences are almost always positive for me, as the most important thing to me is that we do it. My wife, on the other hand, has an image of our family that is more tied to the nature of family interactions and dynamics. For her, it is not so important what activity we are doing as it is that the interactions are harmonious, and it is only leisure if these conditions are met. Skiing in the Rocky Mountains on a beautiful clear spring day with perfect snow is meaningless to her if the kids are whining or there is tension between the two of us.

Likewise, our most satisfying, fulfilling, rewarding moments—our moments of positive self-expression—do not always occur during the "remains of the day," outside of the traditional categories of work and maintenance. Many of us experience a high level of satisfaction on the job, and many of our hours at work are more enjoyable than our free time. Some may even feel guilty that they would rather be at work, where they can focus on rewarding projects, than at home, where family life can be tense and chaotic. Why are these pleasurable and desirable experiences in the workplace not regarded as leisure?

The Time Budget Study

The deeply entrenched categorization of leisure as the time remaining once obligations are met severely limits our ability to define, and hence experience, leisure. A basic tool of leisure research nicely illustrates these limitations: the time budget study. Since the 1960s, time budget studies have been used to measure how much free time we have in which to experience leisure.

Try this easy and revealing time budget study on yourself. Using the form provided at the end of this chapter, record your activities at 30-minute intervals throughout at least one full day. Then, in the column provided, categorize these activities as work, maintenance or leisure. Work refers to paid labor. Maintenance is a broad category that includes all subsistence activity (child care, eldercare, household chores, repairs, cooking, grocery shopping, commuting, etc.) whether it is personal, household or other. Leisure is anything that is neither of the other two. This typical form should show you how much or how little free time you have. More importantly, from the point of view of rediscovering leisure in your life, it will show you how difficult it is to categorize leisure based on time, and you may begin to feel that it will remain elusive if we persist with this kind of leisure definition.

Students in my Leisure Studies classes are required to work through a time budget study in order to begin thinking about leisure in everyday life. Each student is asked to record and then categorize her or his activities for two complete days (24-hour periods), ideally using one weekday and one weekend day. Keep in mind that the purpose of the exercise is to isolate leisure, based on a traditional and popularly accepted definition, whereby *leisure is the time remaining after one's work and maintenance responsibilities have been addressed.* This definition assumes that our day-to-day work, maintenance and leisure activities are clearly different.

According to students, the activity of eating breakfast on a weekday is maintenance, yet on a weekend morning it becomes leisure. Walking the dog is leisure most days, except on days when it is raining or very cold, when it is unquestionably maintenance. Schoolwork is viewed as maintenance for some, work for others (who think of school as their job), and leisure for still others. Likewise driving, or any form of commuting, is an activity that can be found in any of the three categories, depending on the purpose (work, pleasure, etc.) of the trip, the mode of transportation (driving, cycling, walking or taking the bus), and the state of mind (distracted, worried, calm, peaceful) at the time. While gardening can be the perfect leisure experience for some people, it is just another (sometimes unpleasant) job around the house for others.

After performing your own time budget study, you will have a good indication of how you spend your time. But you will also have come to realize how difficult it is to divide life's activities up into rigid categories. Time budget studies are good at telling us how we use our time, but they are not so good at telling us what leisure is. Even an activity such as walking to work can mean something different to different people and even to the same person under different circumstances.

Conducting your own time budget study will help you to realize that the personal meaning of the time is much more relevant in terms of satisfaction and enjoyment than the type of activity. This is a relatively simple conclusion, but I urge you to try the study for yourself for a full appreciation of what it reveals. For most people, it seems reasonable to assume that the leisure part of our day can be isolated, and by conducting the study for yourself, you will begin to see what experiences actually feel like leisure to you, and put you on the path to rediscovery.

Measuring Leisure—Have We Really Lost It?

Leisure is important in and of itself and symbolizes a progressive society, so it is not surprising that we attempt to measure the amount of leisure we have. Leisure predictions generally assume that if we have free time, we also have leisure, and that we would be able to notice *real* quality of life changes resulting from changes in free time. Time budget studies operate with the assumption that leisure is essentially about time; however, while time budget studies are able to measure our *use* of time, they do not measure the amount of satisfaction or enjoyment we get from different types of activities. This is like using a mathematical formula to calculate happiness or love. The idea that leisure can be measured as free time makes more sense on paper than it does in reality. Leisure is too complex and personal to be captured within the rigid categories of the time budget studies.

In order to measure leisure we need to have a benchmark definition of leisure. But we have not, as yet, decided upon a definition that makes sense to all or even most of us. Because we lack a widely accepted definition of leisure, it is quite easy to draw a range of divergent conclusions about the state of our everyday leisure and whether it is increasing or decreasing. Also, without a hard and fast definition, sweeping but probably erroneous assumptions can be made about how almost any trend has impact on leisure. For example, if we know that most of us are working longer hours today, we might conclude that people must be experiencing less leisure. Or, if we discovered that more and more women are in the workforce and they still do about the same amount of housework as in previous decades, then we might say that women must have less leisure in their lives today. On the other hand, if the dollars spent on holiday travel or sporting goods are used as a measure of leisure, we would surely conclude that our leisure is definitely increasing, and that we have far more leisure in our lives today than we have had in the past.

American sociologist Juliet Schor, in her book *The Overworked American*, claims that Americans are working significantly more now than in the past, and therefore experiencing less leisure time. Others, including leisure specialist Geoffrey Godbey, have claimed that leisure time is on the rise. In Canada, Jack Harper's research has revealed that two in five

Canadians feel they have less leisure time now than in the past five years, and only one in five feel they have more leisure time. One of the most comprehensive long-term studies conducted, involving people from several countries, concluded that even though some people have gained leisure in the past several decades, most people—those who work for a living—have lost it.

It is obviously difficult to measure leisure, and to determine how much of it we have in our lives, in the absence of a good definition. Leisure as free time is an arbitrary and over-simplified labeling of a complex and important part of our lives, one that is more subjective than it is objective. It is clear that we need a common way to view leisure if we are to avoid some of the pitfalls of past predictions, and if we are to succeed in rediscovering leisure in our lives today.

Less Leisure in Our Integrated Lives

If we equate leisure with free time, we clearly have much less of it than we did back when the leisure-boom predictions were made. Free time has become one of the biggest casualties of our hyper-paced lives. One of the reasons that we seem to have less free time is that our lives are less compartmentalized. For many of us, the boundaries between work life and non-work life are blurred. In some ways, the personal computer is a good example of the changes we've experienced and the new focus we've come to adopt. When computers first came about, they were strictly tools for work, but today we use them for work, learning, entertainment and personal communication. Flexibility in the workplace enables us to conduct some personal business during the day and electronic communication in the form of home computers and fax machines make it easy—even compelling—to work at home. Products and services aimed at the home office are flourishing. Having a high-speed Internet connection into the computer in the family room might make it easier to handle business and professional communication in our own time frame. But by the same token, the pressure to check the e-mail, and to respond to e-mail messages, can come to feel ever-present and overwhelming (especially if we are efficient, or foolish, enough to set our computers to beep every time we have a new message).

Technology and other forces are blurring the lines separating our time at work, home, school, child care and so on, to the point where free time (in terms of leisure time) is becoming a meaningless concept. Our lives are much more integrated, and on the surface this seems to suggest a hopeless situation, in which we have, and will continue to have, less leisure. This is certainly true if we continue to see leisure as something that is fundamentally about time. The good news is that leisure is *not* about time, and once we recognize this, and define it more experientially, we may find that we actually have much more of it. But we have to stop looking for it in all the wrong places.

Redefining Leisure—The Key to Rediscovery

If leisure is not about time, then what is it about? Certainly we could list several adjectives that describe any pleasant activity or experience, and these do help us to think about what is underlying leisure. Leisure moments can be relaxing, rejuvenating, invigorating, satisfying, rewarding—in short, they make us feel good. But it is a dynamic and deeply personal concept, and most of us harbor one or more strong associations with leisure that help us define it at any given moment. Leisure is not so much about time as it is about *the personal meaning of time,* and the meaning will change over time, as we change. Depending on where we are in our personal journey through life, we may seek experiences that are calming and relaxing, or experiences that are demanding and invigorating. A leisure experience is one that is satisfying, enjoyable and meaningful to you or me as an individual. Identifying the essence of leisure will help each one of us to understand why leisure seems to have disappeared from our lives, and at the same time help us to see that it lives on in other, sometimes unrecognized places. More importantly, once we understand what leisure really is, we will be well on our way to rediscovering it in our lives, and throughout our lives.

Time Budget Study

This is a two-part exercise you can do any time to get a better understanding of how you use your time and what leisure means to you in everyday life.

Part 1: Record your time

1. Record your activity for each time slot provided. Record a complete weekday and weekend day.

2. Indicate in the appropriate column whether the majority of the activity is work, maintenance or leisure (as per the definitions below).

Work—includes all paid labor

Maintenance—includes activities such as sleeping, eating, cleaning, household labor, care of others and the like

Leisure—any time not spent in one of the above categories

Part 2: Think about your results

1. At this time, how would you define leisure? Just think of an understanding of leisure that you may have been using in the past and could use even now to help define leisure.

2. Look at the third column of each time sheet where you labeled your activities as either work, maintenance or leisure. Ask yourself if the labels you gave to the activities are truly representative of the activities in column 2.

You may find that the labels in column 3 are truly reflective of the activities in column 2. You may find that the labels are not representative of the activities. This exercise should give you an idea of how realistic it is to label our leisure as free time.

Time Budget Analysis—Weekday   Date: _____

(1) Time Period	(2) Activity	(3) Work/Maintenance/ Leisure
1200–1230		
1230–0100		
0100–0130		
0130–0200		
0200–0230		
0230–0300		
0300–0330		
0330–0400		
0400–0430		
0430–0500		
0500–0530		
0530–0600		
0600–0630		
0630–0700		
0700–0730		
0730–0800		
0800–0830		
0830–0900		
0900–0930		
0930–1000		
1000–1030		
1030–1100		
1100–1130		

It's Not About Time!

(1) Time Period	(2) Activity	(3) Work/Maintenance/Leisure
1130–1200		
1200–1230		
1230–1300		
1300–1330		
1330–1400		
1400–1430		
1430–1500		
1500–1530		
1530–1600		
1600–1630		
1630–1700		
1700–1730		
1730–1800		
1800–1830		
1830–1900		
1900–1930		
1930–2000		
2000–2030		
2030–2100		
2100–2130		
2130–2200		
2200–2230		
2300–2330		
2330–2400		

Time Budget Analysis–Weekend Day   Date: _____

(1) Time Period	(2) Activity	(3) Work/Maintenance/ Leisure
1200–1230		
1230–0100		
0100–0130		
0130–0200		
0200–0230		
0230–0300		
0300–0330		
0330–0400		
0400–0430		
0430–0500		
0500–0530		
0530–0600		
0600–0630		
0630–0700		
0700–0730		
0730–0800		
0800–0830		
0830–0900		
0900–0930		
0930–1000		
1000–1030		
1030–1100		
1100–1130		

It's Not About Time!

(1) Time Period	(2) Activity	(3) Work/Maintenance/Leisure
1130–1200		
1200–1230		
1230–1300		
1300–1330		
1330–1400		
1400–1430		
1430–1500		
1500–1530		
1530–1600		
1600–1630		
1630–1700		
1700–1730		
1730–1800		
1800–1830		
1830–1900		
1900–1930		
1930–2000		
2000–2030		
2030–2100		
2100–2130		
2130–2200		
2200–2230		
2300–2330		
2330–2400		

Chapter References

Edginton, Christopher; Jordan, Debra, J.; DeGraaf, Donald G.; Edginton, Susan R. 1995. *Leisure and Life Satisfaction.* Dubuque, IA: Brown & Benchmark Publishers.

Harper, Jack; Neider, Denny; Godbey, Geoffrey; and Lamont, Darlene. 1997. "The Use & Benefits of Local Government Parks & Recreation Services" (Executive Summary). Presented at the 1997 Canadian Parks & Recreation Conference in St. John's NF. (This references has further details on the 1997 survey on Canadians and leisure referred to in this chapter.)

Kelly, John. 1989. "Leisure Behaviors and Styles: Social, Economic, and Cultural Analysis." In *Understanding Leisure and Recreation: Mapping the Past, Charting the Future.* State College, PA: Venture Publishing Inc.

Perlstein, Rick. 1997. "Field Notes: Leisure World." *Lingua Franca.*

Samuel, Nicole. 1996. "Technology Invades Leisure." *Leisure and Recreation,* World Leisure and Recreation Association. Vol. 38, No. 3.

Zuzanek, Jiri; Beckers, Theo; and Peters, Pascale. 1998. "The 'Harried' Class Revisited: Dutch and Canadian Trends in the Use of Time from the 1970s to the 1990s." *Leisure Studies,* Vol. 17.

• Chapter 2 •

In Search of Leisure

Somewhere in North America (where there's snow) on a Monday morning in December, Rick and Larry are at work and discussing their respective weekends.

"So Rick, what did you do this weekend?" asked Larry, rather quietly.

"Susan and I stayed home, hung out around the house, did a little bit of work and caught a movie on Saturday night," replied Rick.

"So how was it?" continued Larry.

"It was great, just what we needed, you know...very relaxed. It was great," said Rick. "How about you, Larry, didn't you and Gail take the kids skiing? How was that?"

"My family hates me," Larry replied, staring into his coffee cup.

"Hates you? How can they hate you after you took them skiing for the weekend?" asked a surprised Rick. "What makes you think they hate you?"

"Oh, they do. I can tell; I could see it in their eyes all the way home last night," replied Larry.

Rick continued questioning. "How do you know they hate you? What'd they say?"

"Nothing; they haven't talked to me since we left the rental shop," answered Larry.

"What could you have possibly done to make them hate you?" asked Rick incredulously.

"I'm not sure...the whole thing is still a bit of a blur, but I did have good intentions—I had really good intentions," Larry continued, "I thought it was time to teach the kids to ski. You know, Rick, I've been patiently waiting for the kids to be old enough to ski. I've always seen us as a ski-ing kind of family. Gail said we should put them into lessons, but I thought I could teach them and make it a family thing. You know, I used to be a pretty hot skier before Gail and I had the kids. I've skied my share of bumps."

"So what happened?" inquired Rick.

"I think Gail was right," replied Larry. "It sort of went from bad from to worse. The kids didn't catch on quite as fast as I thought they would, and the more I tried to teach, the worse it got."

"So did you lose your cool?" asked Rick.

"Oh, everybody got so frustrated, but I had no idea just how frustrated until Gail asked the ski patrol to put me on 'time-out' at the bottom of the tow rope so the kids could calm down."

"A ski-patrol?" repeated Rick. "Were any other authorities involved?"

"No, of course not," Larry said. "Well, some young ski instructor said I was banned from teaching on that hill forever."

"Boy, that sounds like a great weekend," quipped Rick.

Larry continued to stare into his cup. He stirred and slowly said, "I have no idea how such a good thing like a ski weekend could go so horribly."

"So what are you going to do?" asked Rick, thinking that therapy might be Larry's response.

"I booked the kids into a no-parent ski camp for the holidays," said Larry.

This conversation illustrates some of the ways we all search for and experience—or fail to experience—leisure. Rick and Larry, like all of us, are constantly searching for leisure in their own ways. It appears that Rick found leisure in his relaxed weekend with his partner and Larry thought he was on the right track with his family ski trip. While his heart was in the right place, Larry's weekend was anything but a leisure experi-ence. In fact, it was miserable for everyone. We all have our own ways of defining leisure in any given moment, and sometimes just being involved in what we would consider "leisure activity" does not result in what feels like a leisure experience.

The Search Begins

Let's begin the search for a definition of leisure with what we know. We know that we all experience leisure in one way or another, whether as free time, play, a holiday, a few days of rest and relaxation, or a simple feeling of joy and excitement within *any* activity. Recognizing that there are many different ways of thinking about and experiencing leisure is critical to rediscovering it in our lives.

The way that we define leisure at any given moment is through vague associations most of us already have with the word "leisure." Though our associations may be vague—most of us don't spend a lot of time actually thinking about these associations—they intuitively guide our daily search for leisure. Some of the more common associations include leisure as free time, leisure as time away from work, leisure as recreation and travel, leisure as balance and leisure as idleness. Each association explains a part of what leisure is but not one of them, on its own, gives us a complete picture. By exploring each of these traditional leisure associations in more detail, we can become aware of our own deep-seated assumptions about leisure and how they may facilitate or impede our ability to experience it.

Leisure as Free Time

One of our most limited resources and precious possessions is time—and more importantly, free time. As precious as it is, there is a very good chance we'll be disappointed if we expect our free time to translate into our leisure. Yet most of us still associate free time with leisure. The shortcoming of this association is that it implies that if we don't have free time we don't have leisure. One reason many of us continue to think of leisure as free time is that it is easy to measure in terms of our daily scheduling. As we saw in the time budget studies discussed in Chapter 1, we can measure the amount of free time we have available on any given day.

What is it about time that makes it such a precious and limited resource? Like leisure, time is a very complex concept and one that is difficult to define. Everyone knows what time is until we are asked to define it. We have forgotten that in high school physics we were taught that time is the measurement of an object traveling through space. But time is much more meaningful to us, on a day-to-day basis, than this definition is able to capture. Much of what time means to us is cultural. Time is not just a physical property; it is a socially constructed one. Some of us are not aware that there are many different ways of perceiving time which have direct implications for our experience of it. In many Eastern societies, time is considered to be cyclical, and it can be recycled. No moment is lost forever, but can be retrieved in some way in the future. In North America, however, we have a very different, linear model of time. We think of time as non-cyclical, whereby once a moment is lived it can never be retrieved—it is lost forever. This concept of time makes it a valuable commodity that, like a precious stone, we end up trying to buy, sell, trade, or even steal on a daily basis.

What makes time even more precious is that we can generally do only *one* thing at a time. When you are at work, you can't get to any of the chores around the house. When you're doing laundry, you're not playing with the kids, and when you're stuck in traffic and your cellphone battery just died, you're stuck in traffic. When we can only do one thing at a time, we sometimes feel as though we are paying a price for that restriction. That price is called opportunity cost, which, from a business or economic point of view, refers to the fact that resources directed in one area cannot be directed elsewhere. By virtue of taking advantage of one opportunity, you lose another. With reference to time, opportunity cost refers to the cost of not being able to do all the things we would like to—having to choose *one* of many options.

Refusal to accept the "one thing at a time" limitation has led to widespread multi-tasking. Multi-tasking—doing two or more things at one time—has come to be seen as a way (sometimes the only way) to get more things done, and thus relieve some of our time stress. It was one of the key tools of early time management strategies. Multi-tasking occurs when we try to watch the kids while making supper, carry on a conversation while balancing the checkbook, talk on the phone while driving, or in some cases, interact with the kids while having a telephone conversation while checking e-mail while listening to the news. But multi-tasking is at the very least a double-edged sword. In may even be a deal with the devil. Because while it may make us more efficient in the short term, it can contribute significantly to stress and the long-term health consequences of stress, to an inability to focus, and an inability to experience satisfaction in any of the tasks we are undertaking. Multi-tasking, for many people, is incompatible with being fully present in the moment, fully focused on the task at hand. Full focus on the task at hand or in the present moment is an essential element of the kind of deeply satisfying experience that is referred to as "flow" (discussed further in Chapter 3). But this too is highly individual. Some people thrive in a multi-tasking situation, feeling vibrant and alive in a way that others can only feel while hiking a mountain pass. Whether multi-tasking is a successful solution that creates more leisure in your life, or a significant threat to your ability to be present in the moment and thus experience leisure, is something that each individual must decide.

Given the mountain of demands we all face, the pace of life and the value of time, it's no wonder we consider ourselves to be time-stressed. About half of all North Americans experience moderate to high levels of stress in trying to balance their jobs and home life. That figure has doubled over the past 10 years and there is no sign of its decreasing in the future. Recent studies reported that about four out of five of us describe feeling sometimes or always rushed. Not surprisingly, it is estimated that two in five North Americans have less leisure time now than five years ago.

Most of us believe that we face too many demands on our time on any given day, and this sense of being overwhelmed—of constantly swimming up-river—results in time stress. Unfortunately, the obligations in our day usually take precedence over the other things we would like to do. It is not difficult to fill a given day with obligations to the point where there is nothing left at the end. This means that if we think of leisure as being free time, leisure time would likely be the leftover part of the day, and yet for most of us, there is no leftover part of the day, or if there is, we are too exhausted to enjoy it.

Another reason the leisure and time association does not work is that we cannot clearly separate the work, maintenance and leisure times of our lives in a meaningful way. We have seen that any one activity can mean something different at different times. The experience of time is very subjective, so it is no wonder that we run into problems when we begin to assume that leisure is only found in our free time and that all free time must be leisure. Leslie Bella, a Leisure Studies professor in Canada, believes that the personal meaning of the time is far more relevant than the activity itself. She has pointed out how the same free time situation, such as a festive dinner, can be a completely different experience for men and women. Men generally find these occasions to be relaxed and enjoyable, while women experience less relaxation and enjoyment due to stress over meal preparation and even tension management during the meal. But again, this depends on the individual talents and self-images of the persons involved. Some women find they are most fulfilled while handling a large, complex and stressful family dinner. Likewise, some men might find it stressful if they do not have an active contribution to make to such an occasion.

Free, unobligated time is a popular association that we have with leisure, but by itself it does not do justice to the personal side of the leisure experience, which does not always occur when we have free time, and which can occur during obligated time, such as time at work. Work is the traditional opposite of leisure. Many of us may actually experience feelings of satisfaction, rejuvenation and enjoyment while working. What do you feel when you've overcome a major challenge at work, or when you are recognized for a job well done? Is this really any different from the feeling we get after a great drive off the tee or playing a complete piece on the piano perfectly? Leisure is not about time: it is about the personal meaning of the time.

Leisure versus Work

Another very common and related association we make with leisure is that leisure is time *not* spent at work (where work is considered paid labor). This view, however, is quickly becoming outdated. We all know at least one person (if not ourselves) who loves their work so much that there is no real difference between their work and their leisure. Indeed, for some, work can be the primary source of satisfaction, rejuvenation and pleasure.

Many of the earlier definitions of leisure were based on the idea that leisure and work were opposites. Stanley Parker, one of the fathers of

Leisure Studies, defined leisure as time not spent at work. The Economic Model of Leisure asserted that leisure is the time remaining after work and maintenance responsibilities are met. In each case, leisure is considered to be distinctly different from work.

We have arrived at the leisure and work association through centuries of reinforcement. The leisured class of the 16th, 17th and 18th centuries was made up of those wealthy few who did not have to work and lived a life of luxury. The rest of the population—the working class—was left to work in the fields and mines and, later on, the factories to support themselves. The Industrial Revolution conjures up images of harsh working conditions, long hours and even child labor that today would be considered little better than slavery. The work-as-drudgery image continued through recent history, with unions' demands for humane working conditions in the early 1900s, the poverty and dust-bowl conditions of the Depression, and even the robot-like manufacturing employee of the 1950s. The image of work we have inherited at the turn of the millennium is that work is a non-negotiable obligation, so lacking in satisfaction that its opposite—leisure—must be something good and valued. While today we recognize that serious efforts have been made to increase personal job satisfaction, the work-as-drudgery image continues, if to a lesser degree.

The simplicity of defining our leisure today strictly as time away from work falls short for at least two reasons. First, leisure and work are not the opposites they once were. We can no longer say that all time at work is drudgery and all time away from work is enjoyable. As noted above, some people get more satisfaction and enjoyment from their work than their non-work time. For many of us, there is no clear line separating work and leisure in terms of the satisfaction gained. There is no rule that the activities related to work and career cannot be just as satisfying, enjoyable and personally rewarding as any typical leisure activity.

The second problem with the leisure versus work opposition is that this view of leisure excludes those who are not part of the paid labor force. It implies that only those who work for pay have the right to claim leisure at the end of the day. Are women or men who stay home to manage the household and care for children living a life of leisure? Or by virtue of working continuously without pay are not entitled to leisure? And what about full-time students? Or those who operate a home business? The leisure-work association helps us narrow our understanding of what leisure is and what leisure is not, but due to the blurred boundaries between work and leisure today, it fails to capture the broader meaning of leisure.

Leisure as Idleness

Suppose you decide one Saturday to do nothing, to vegetate, to be a couch potato. Is this leisure? Within our fast-paced world, a little down time with nothing to do may be just what many of us are looking for. Leisure in the form of idleness is precisely what Rick and his partner were seeking in the narrative. They were trying to escape from their hectic daily routines with a quiet, slow-moving weekend.

Our historic image of the non-working, wealthy leisured class brought about a non-productive and largely negative association with the term "idleness." It was thought to be destructive to the moral fiber of a society. The Puritans of early America, with their Protestant work ethic, thought that idleness was the root of all evil. The lingering effects of the Protestant work ethic explain, at least in part, why many people still feel guilty about being idle. We continue to think of idleness as a waste of time when, today, time has become so precious. It's not surprising that people who find themselves involuntarily unemployed experience the stress and often guilt of being non-productive. Most of us can sit idle for only so long before anxiety sets in. Further, if under-stimulation is a challenge that we face, then idleness is hardly going to produce the desired effect.

The leisure as idleness association illustrates only one side of leisure; that is, the "escape" side. Escaping the stress of everyday pressures is the whole point of idleness, but it holds different meanings for different people. It can be the perfect form of escape if we are on a tropical beach and feel that we have earned it, or it can be very stressful if it is in some way forced upon us. Idleness, or simple down time, represents an important but narrow aspect of leisure. Associating leisure with idleness can bring about the same result as eating one too many pieces of chocolate: satisfying one craving only to feel guilty in the end.

We return to Rick who, on that same day, is having lunch with Lisa and Barb, his two co-workers.

"Why is Larry so down?" asked Lisa.

"His family hates him," said Rick in a matter-of-fact tone. "He did the I-father-teach-you-child-to-ski thing and it blew up in his face."

"Didn't he just do the I-father-teach-you-child-to-swim thing and have that backfire too?" asked Barb.

"Yes, but to this day he swears that the lifeguard was overreacting."

Lisa burst in with, "Well, my weekend was just great!"

"What did you do?" asked both Barb and Rick, looking up from their food.

"I did absolutely nothing and it was awesome," said a proud Lisa. She continued, "You have to understand that it's been a long, long time since I've done nothing. Ever since September I've been just going, going, going. If it's not work, or stuff around the house, it's Jane's dance or Brad's hockey and Scouts. Or it's the fund-raising Bingos for dance, hockey and Scouts. And it's those early bird fitness classes that I'm still going to only because they cost me a fortune, and this weekly stress management class is killing me. I'm spread so thin that if I get one more person demanding something from me I'm going to explode."

"I hear you saying you're too busy," said Rick, half-sarcastic and half-afraid of where she was going with this.

"No Rick, it's not just being busy, everybody's busy. I'm spread too thin, doing too many things, and I don't feel like I have the time or energy to do any of them well...except, of course, for the new account you gave me, Barb," said Lisa, smiling at her supervisor. She continued, "Do you know what it's like to read The English Patient three sentences at a time?"

Rick and Barb gestured no with mouths full.

"Well, let me tell you, some of the romance is lost when someone's calling for you every two minutes. I can't even tell you what part of the book I'm at. And reading at night doesn't work because I go from being on duty to being asleep. There's no energy to do anything in between."

"Nothing?" asked Rick, surprised. "Really?"

"Nothing," said Lisa and Barb together.

"My mother once told me that being a parent is the best contraceptive," said Rick, happy to be able to contribute.

"Well, she's right," replied Lisa.

"Your mother said that to you?" replied Barb, to no response. She continued, *"I can see why you loved your 'doing nothing' weekend, but I have to tell you when I was on maternity leave I went crazy. I couldn't stand the singular focus of being at home. It just doesn't work for me."*

"You see, I loved that part of being on maternity leave," said Lisa.

Barb put down her sandwich and continued, *"I almost lost my mind. I was more than ready to come back after six months home with Jesse, and a little less so after the second time with Stardust, but still I was itching to get back. I'm afraid to say it out loud sometimes, but I just love being busy and having lots of different things going on, like work, which is great right now, and the kids' stuff and the ladies' hiking club, and I think I'm going to start teaching one night a week at the college next term."*

"How do you do it?" asked a suddenly exhausted Lisa.

"I do get tired," answered Barb, *"but I also get energized by doing so many different things. Who knows, maybe I'll burn out, but it's really great right now."*

Rick added, *"For me work is work. It's just a job. But from where I sit at least both of you have lives. You should see my wife Susan. Ever since her company was bought out and went global it seems they're working around the clock. Everyone there is just scrambling to make their new quotas. I'm sure that Susan can't even spell the word l-i-f-e any more."*

All the while, Lisa listened attentively and then added, *"You know what I wonder about? I wonder about how much of this treadmill we actually choose, and how much just sneaked up on us when we weren't paying attention?"*

"Well, Lisa," concluded Rick, *"you're still alive so you've got some choices ahead of you, and I now choose to eat my lunch."*

Leisure as Balance

"Leisure as balance" might make you think of quality of life or a holistic approach to living, or simply living a lifestyle based on the adage "variety is the spice of life." But leisure and balance share a common element: choice. Leisure implies that we have the freedom to make choices about what we do, as does the concept of balance. Achieving a balanced lifestyle is a significant goal for many North Americans.

Balance is important for those who want diversity in life, and it is one of the ways we tend to look for leisure. Most of us recognize that we can find satisfaction, enjoyment and even energy from a variety of sources in daily life. It's naive to believe that we are exclusively rejuvenated by one part of our lives, whether at home, work or play. We find satisfaction and energy in recreation, sports, community work, reading a book, playing with children, visiting friends, paid work, evening classes and many other areas of life. Leisure as balance is about being able to pick and choose where we find our satisfaction, yet remain in control of our lives.

Most of us want to avoid a situation in which one part of our life dominates to the exclusion of other parts. Work, parenting, school or even volunteer activities can take over at the expense of other important aspects of our lives. This situation represents an imbalance. It's the type of thing that I hear about when I talk to workaholics, or students who have just graduated and want to begin leading a "normal" life, or parents who are just getting beyond the kids-in-diapers stage and want to rejoin the world. Most of us have an ideal of a life that is rich in meaning, relationships, resources, activity and relaxation. Few of us set out to undertake lives with but a single purpose, even though in the short term, putting all of our eggs in one basket can be rewarding and is often encouraged. A generation of men, caught up in the consumerism and economic opportunities of the '80s and '90s, dedicated themselves almost exclusively to work during the critical career-building years between 25 and 45. Many then discovered that their children were grown and had not waited for them to be ready to participate, or that their health had suffered as a result of overwork, or that personal relationships had atrophied through neglect. Balance is an important aspect of a life that includes real leisure.

While leisure as balance is a central notion in the 21st century, the idea has been with us for centuries. The ancient Greek ideal of the complete man was based on balance. The noblemen of the Renaissance encouraged a balanced view of the world through the liberalization of the arts, sciences and social activities. However, in North America, the association between leisure and balance has been most greatly shaped by events of the past three decades.

Since the end of World War II, we have experienced countless changes to North American society. The 1950s were a time of optimism and clarity, and everyone seemed to know their roles in society. Children went to school, mothers stayed at home, dads went to work, governments provided schooling, and health and industry created wealth. The expectations of each group were clear and well understood by everyone. By the 1970s, this had all changed. Wages dropped, unemployment and inflation rose and people began questioning everything, including their roles and the relevance of major institutions like government, marriage and religion. Many changes occurred at this time, but the change that most affected leisure and balance was the shift in our traditional roles.

All of a sudden women raised children, kept house, went to college and began careers. Men still went to work as they had in the past, but they had expanded roles at home (to a lesser degree than women). All conventions were broken: people returned to school as mature students, began taking second jobs, went on maternity leave and men even stayed home while their wives went to work. On television, female role models evolved from June Cleaver to Mary Tyler Moore. It's no wonder Archie Bunker had such a hard time trying to make sense of the world.

Today, we are no longer stuck in any one role and we can wear as many different hats as we want to, or can manage. Often we wear these different hats by choice because at some level, we know that the potential for overall satisfaction rests in many different parts of our world. Sometimes we are forced to wear a number of different hats, perhaps as a single parent or simply because of the pressure to be accomplished in different areas. Both men and women feel the pressure to constantly upgrade their skills, while statistics continue to show how important it is for parents to spend more time with their children.

We're constantly being pulled in different directions and each demand seems to claim the highest priority. It's no wonder we are time-stressed, and we may feel we are running full speed just to be able to stay in the race. As a population, we may be doing well relatively speaking, but doing well means doing more work with what feels like less satisfaction. The heart of Lisa's frustration in the narrative is that she is constantly overwhelmed by the daily demands of doing well. For many of us, wearing a number of hats is exactly what we are looking for, but the danger lies in sacrificing the amount of satisfaction we get from each role.

The leisure as balance association is important because it highlights the aspect of leisure based on our freedom to pursue all those experiences we believe will bring us closer to our full capacity. It does not matter whether those experiences are in the home, play, community or work parts of our lives. On the other hand, leisure as balance falls short as a useful benchmark because balance is too ambiguous and hard to control.

Few of us can strictly regulate the amount of time and energy we dedicate to any one part of life. Most of the time we are "flying by the seat of our pants" and dealing with issues as they arise. Just when we make plans, life happens and scuttles them. Life is dynamic and even though we may desire balance, we cannot always control or maintain it. And we cannot forget that the road to balance is a slippery one that can lead to the kind of over-commitment that plagues Lisa in our multi-tasking society. At the same time, Barb thrives on a life of balanced diversity.

Leisure as Recreation

Hopscotch, golf, reading, bicycling, tennis, a warm-weather getaway in mid-winter, a camping trip... Undoubtedly, one of the most powerful associations we have with leisure is that it equates to a recreational activity or a vacation. The term recreation covers a broad range of activities that includes sports, play, reading, the arts and pleasure travel. Research indicates that walking for pleasure and bicycling are the most popular everyday recreational activities.

How we spend our recreation time and money, and how much of these we invest in recreation, is generally a good reflection of who we are, or how we see ourselves. Knowing what someone does in their free time, or what they do with their disposable income, will tell you much more about who the person really is than knowing what they do for a living. How much does Bob's job in the oil and gas industry tell you about Bob? Probably not much. Knowing how Bob spends his Saturdays will likely tell you much more.

Does he sit in his favorite chair all day and watch old movies on Nickelodeon? Does he spend the time with his children in an array of child-centered activities? Does he spend it in a solitary activity such as refurbishing an antique car? Or does he sit in a blues tavern with his friends listening to the weekly blues jam? Recreation is strongly associated with leisure, and for good reason. Recreational activities are supposed to be self-directed and self-fulfilling, and as such they reinforce the image we hold of ourselves. We can and do receive great satisfaction and enjoyment through recreation and vacationing. I know people who live for this part of life—they plan their work lives to support their play.

Recreation activities have two central defining elements: they happen within the parameters of a certain time and a certain space—the afternoon (time) of golf at the golf course (space), the evening (time) of tennis at the tennis court (space), the afternoon (time) walk or bike ride in the park (space), or the midwinter (time) trip to the Caribbean (space). Each of these typical forms of recreation includes a time and a space element. Time and space are defining characteristics of leisure as recreation—they are what tell us, at least in part, that it is a recreation activity we're doing. We tend to think of recreation and vacation activity as being different and separate from other activities in everyday life. We could be having just as much fun and satisfaction at work or at school, but we don't think of it as recreation because it's not happening in the "recreation" time and space.

Since the time of the ancient Greeks and Romans, there have been similarities in how we think of play, recreation and leisure. The word "recreation" originated during the Renaissance from the term "re-creation," implying rejuvenation. Rejuvenation became important to the working classes, as it allowed them to better withstand the rigors of harsh working conditions. Recreation activities of that era were not so different from recreation activities of today. Card games, sports, the arts, travel for pleasure and going to pubs made up some of the more popular activities of the day. During the Renaissance, as today, recreation activity existed apart from the requirements of daily life, specifically to serve the purpose of rejuvenation.

Today we still think of leisure as recreation activity. Recreation and vacation activities are by far the easiest of all leisure activities to identify and measure. As well, from an early age we are schooled in the difference between recreation activities and other activities. Schools tend to isolate the recreation-based curriculum, taught in physical education or arts classes, from the rest of the curriculum. A minor point perhaps, but it serves to reinforce the idea that recreation occurs within its own time and space, and the idea that we still use recreation as a means of rejuvenation.

The leisure as recreation association is important because we have a common belief that recreation and travel play an important role in bringing about the leisure experience. However, this association possesses two shortcomings that prevent us from using it as our benchmark.

By now we are all aware that the fact that we are participating in a recreation activity does not guarantee that it will be a true leisure experience. In the narrative, Larry and his family were skiing within a vacation setting, and they did not even come close to experiencing leisure—they were all too frustrated. Most of us have had experiences like Larry's family ski trip. My family has only recently started hiking in the mountains again because on the first few trips, I was a Larry in hiking boots. Recreation does not necessarily result in a leisure experience. Despite the saying "a bad day on the golf course is better than a good day at the office," in reality this is not always the case. A child who is pressured into sports or music against her or his will is not likely to enjoy anything about the experience. Recreation and travel do not *always* result in a positive leisure experience.

A second problem with equating leisure with recreation is the time- and space-bound nature of recreation and recreational travel. This is a far too limiting definition of leisure, which we know can be found almost anywhere, any time. Identifying leisure with recreation eliminates too many of the times and places where leisure must necessarily occur. The potential for rediscovering leisure would be severely constrained for many of us who do not have the time, money, inclination or physical ability to engage in regular recreational activities or travel.

What Leisure Is Not

Each of the associations discussed tells us something about what leisure is and what it is not. None, in and of itself, is able to fully capture the essence of leisure. Leisure is related to, but different from, each of these associations. In summary, and before we embark on an exploration of what leisure is, it is clear that leisure is not simply:

- Leftover time at the end of the day, once our work and maintenance obligations have been addressed.
- Idleness. Doing nothing may be exactly what we're looking for at times, but idleness only addresses one aspect of leisure.
- A set of activities. A set of recreation or travel activities alone does not constitute our leisure. We know that the satisfying part of these activities is found from the individual meaning of the activity.
- Bound by time and space. Leisure cannot be limited to a set of activities that occur in a specific time and place. We know that we find the effects of leisure outside the walls of traditional leisure, in places such as work, school, at home and beyond.

Chapter References

Bella, Leslie. 1989. "Women and Leisure: Beyond Androcentrism." In *Understanding Leisure and Recreation: Mapping the Past, Charting the Future.* State College, PA: Venture Publishing Inc.

Hamilton Ross Systematics. 1996. *1996 Alberta Recreation Survey.*

Bregha, Francis J. 1991. "Leisure and Freedom Re-examined." In *Recreation and Leisure: Issues in an Era of Change.* State College, PA: Venture Publishing Inc.

Brook, Judith A. 1993. "Leisure Meanings and Comparisons with Work." *Leisure Studies,* Vol. 2.

Jenish, D'Arcy, and Driedger Doyle, Sharon. 1994. "The Time Crunch." *Maclean's,* June 20.

Rechtschaffen, Stephan. 1996. *Time Shifting: Creating More Time to Enjoy Your Life.* New York: Doubleday.

Westland, Cor. 1990. "Leisure in an Emerging Community." *World Leisure and Recreation,* World Leisure and Recreation Association. Vol. 32, No. 1 (Spring).

Chapter 3

Leisure Is

We encountered some of the elements of leisure in each of the leisure associations reviewed in Chapter 2, even though none of these associations—time, work, balance, recreation or idleness—on its own offers a meaningful analogue of leisure for today's world. The time has come for us to rediscover leisure as more than an arbitrary moment of free time.

In this chapter I would like to propose a definition of leisure that will act as our basis for analysis, comparison, contemplation and rediscovery.

Leisure Is...

Leisure is the experience of living a moment of positive self-expression. This definition includes, but is not limited to, any one of the leisure associations we have considered. It is about how we interpret the meaning of the activity during the moment in which it is experienced. This view may force us to rethink everyday leisure; it requires us to look at leisure as something deeply personal. The definition is based on three components that bring all the leisure associations together.

Leisure is an *experience.* It is an experience, rather than free time, or time away from work, or some activity. The time or activity is defined by the personal meaning that it holds. It is highly dynamic and individual. As Leslie Bella pointed out, men and women might experience the same activity, but this activity can bring about significantly different leisure experiences for different people. In leisure, the activity is secondary to our experience of it.

Leisure is *living within a moment*. A basic prerequisite for the leisure experience is a deep awareness and connection with our immediate world. Simple, yet likely more challenging than it appears, given that much of the time our minds are racing to re-analyze the past, or ponder or dream about or fret over the future. Our minds are often racing to the office when we are at home and racing back home when we are at the office. In our leisure we seek to step off the hurried conveyor belt of life to experience the moment, to be fully present here and now. Mindfulness, timeshifting or living in the moment has become widely recognized as an essential but often missing element of our lives today. Several popular books have been written on this subject. It is at the heart of leisure.

Leisure cannot be experienced in the present if the mind is racing through the past or future. Persistent nagging thoughts of the past, future and elsewhere plague some of us continually. Most parents today are all too aware of the fact that while our children clamor for our attention, we are scheming about how we're going to tackle the many tasks we have yet to complete. Many of us feel this way at work. I have a friend who loves her job, but has a poster hanging in her office that reads: **Having a great time, wish I were here.** It's what a typical millennium vacationer—glued to the cellphone and laptop—should be writing on postcards to send home.

There are a number of ways that we are taken out of the present moment and thus prevented from experiencing leisure, regardless of the time, place or activity in which we are involved. Our minds may be trapped in the past, worrying about distant roads not taken or recent words we wish we hadn't spoken. Or we may be trapped in the future, thinking about all that we still have to do, or worrying about an upcoming event or announcement. Or we can be trapped in the out-of-the-moment zone between what we are really experiencing and our expectations of what we should be experiencing. Constantly evaluating whether the moment is what you wanted it to be is one of the most insidious and unrecognized ways that we are robbed of mindfulness and thus leisure. Being fully present in the moment requires that we accept the moment on its own terms, and not wish it were something else.

There is a very practical relationship between leisure, time awareness and satisfaction. For example, people who engage in high-risk activities generally get great satisfaction from these activities, which is the draw in the first place. When you are engaged in an extreme activity, like careening down the side of a mountain on a snowboard, you have little choice but to live in the moment: if you lose your focus, you could lose your life. Vastly different activities, such as tennis, downhill skiing, deadline problem-solving, gourmet cooking, reading and rock climbing can all result in a highly rewarding state of all-consuming clarity. Once engaged, there are no thoughts of yesterday or tomorrow, only of the task at hand. This is the basic allure of these activities—they force mindfulness upon the person engaged in the pursuit. Many who achieve mindfulness through much calmer day-to-day activities may fail to understand the desire to undertake extreme activities, but to its participants, it may be one of the only times they feel fully alive in the present moment. Or it is the only way to achieve such all-consuming clarity and focus. When we engage in these activities, we discover an energizing connectedness and clarity that allows for the experience…of the experience.

Consider your own experiences for a moment. Can you remember a recent free-time experience when you were not mentally present? When you were there in body, but your mind was elsewhere? How satisfying was the experience? Likely, not very. Now try to remember a very different experience, an experience in which you were completely connected to yourself and your surroundings. Your next move, whether mental or physical, was instinctive and perfect. Leisure can only be experienced when we are connected, mindful and given completely to the moment. Therefore *a prerequisite for leisure is not a moment of free time, but rather any moment when we are genuinely connected to our actions and surroundings.*

Leisure is *positive self-expression.* Positive self-expression involves engaging in activities that are in line with your current image of yourself, reinforcing your ideal self-image, whether through behavior, activity or thought. If you think of yourself as a great parent, then most any experience you consider to be great parenting is an act of positive self-expression. If you find yourself approaching midlife and think of yourself as the avid outdoors person that you were 20 years ago, you may be drawn to sign up for some kind of life-affirming, epic-style trek that brings you closer to that image. This concept of "positive self-expression" has no right or wrong, no good or bad. It is highly personal and completely based upon our individual self-image.

To attain positive self-expression, three things are essential. First, we must *have* a self-image, an ideal of who or what we want to be. This self-image is critical because it acts as our internal gauge for satisfaction, pleasure and self-expression. Self-reflection to remain aware of our current self-image is important, as self-image is dynamic and will change over time. Second, we must believe we have the *freedom* to pursue the experiences that reinforce our self-image. Third, whatever these experiences are, they must succeed in bringing us closer to our self-image.

One of the satisfying things about a leisure experience is the sense of accomplishment we feel, whether at play or work. This happens when our desire—and skill—allow us to overcome a meaningful challenge, and we experience deep satisfaction as a result. We really enjoy work when we get it right. We enjoy sports most when we're challenged and still successful. Public speaking becomes bearable and even fun when we're able to over-come our fears enough to be creative and expressive. Playing with children or socializing with friends is satisfying when we feel we genuinely connect and contribute. We crave success in the big things in life as well as the everyday, because it brings us closer to the person we wish to be.

Leisure's most recognizable feature—the feature that tells us we've found it—is the point when we are doing, performing, accomplishing or thinking exactly what we believe we should be; in other words, supporting our ideal self-image. This is clear in the outcome of self-expression. Sometimes this means that work is leisure, if we primarily think of and value ourselves as a hard worker.

Six Pillars of Leisure

There are six basic ideas that support the definition of leisure as an experi-ence of living in a moment of positive self-expression. The first three—free-dom, choice and self-expression—form the concept of leisure. The latter three—arousal, flow and stress avoidance—describe our motivation for seeking leisure.

Freedom

In contemporary research, leisure is commonly described in terms of free-dom. Researchers have pointed out that there is a profound and intimate relationship between leisure and perceived freedom—we are only as free as we think we are. Freedom to do some things, and freedom from other things, are generally considered to be essential components of leisure.

Freedom *from* obligation and drudgery is essential to leisure. Without the sense of freedom from that which is obligatory and necessary in life, we do not experience leisure. However, it's not just work that we need to be freed from, because some of us may love to work. In a broad sense, it is the *necessity* of labor or any non-negotiable obligation that stands between leisure and us. This idea may still be too narrow. A broader scope includes freedom from *anything* that we do only because we *have* to, not because we choose to. For instance, those piano lessons that were forced on you as a kid were not leisure (at the time, anyway); Saturday morning housecleaning is not leisure for most of us, nor is Sunday dinner with the in-laws in some cases.

The other part of the leisure–freedom relationship is based on freedom *to*—freedom to undertake those activities that support our efforts to become the person we want to be and have the ability to become. Freedom to and freedom from are flip sides of the same coin. When we are preoccupied with stress, boredom or anxiety, we are not in a position to achieve our full potential. Freedom from the stress and oppression of daily life and freedom to achieve our full capacity lead to expression of our self-image, regardless of our environmental constraints. Inherent in this idea of freedom is the ability to choose.

Choice

As much as we need freedom for leisure, we also need choice. The common perception of leisure as the ability to "do whatever I want to do" indicates the high value we attribute to choice.

In the course of a normal day, we express our freedom through choice. If we wake up in the morning, quickly scan the day and find every moment committed with obligations largely put in place by others, we feel restricted and cannot make the choices that lead us to self-expression. Making choices is the way we act out our sense of freedom. Therefore, having choices tells us whether or not we have freedom. Realistically, of course, our choices are often limited. But the more choices we have, the more free we feel.

Leisure must include the element of choice or it is just another obligation. Implicit within each leisure association is the idea of choice. Whether it is choosing what we do in our free time or choosing to take part in recreation and travel activities or choosing to do nothing, individual choice is paramount. When the only reward we find in the activity is completely external to ourselves, such as playing the piano *only* to satisfy your mom or working *only* for the pay, it is unlikely that leisure will be experienced.

Self-expression

Freedom and choice lead us to acts of self-expression, and self-expression is the ultimate goal of leisure. We have seen evidence of this throughout history. Whether it was through the ancient Greek expression of the ideal man, or the artistic, scientific and travel advancements of the Renaissance, leisure has been recognizable in its ability to bring about self-expression. Specific activities and concepts of time have changed throughout history, but leisure's role of bringing about self-expression has remained constant.

In order to have self-expression, we need a self-image. Francis Bregha argues that leisure is not possible without this sense of self-image. Freedom to achieve our full potential requires that we have some idea of what our full capacity is, much like the Greeks' ideal man, who was an accomplished warrior, statesman, scholar and diplomat. For example, we have images for common stereotypes. A "super-mom" is a woman who does it all: it is an image to which many women aspire (or at least they did before the costs of doing it all became realized). For men, the same is true in the idea of the "Renaissance man." Our self-image becomes the mental target that guides many of our choices, and leisure is the positive expression of this self-image.

The role of self-image in directing leisure usually becomes apparent in children when they begin to determine their own activities—to choose what they will and will not do, what programs they will register in, whether they will go to summer camp and so on. As children get to know themselves and develop a self-image, they begin to crave opportunities for self-expression to confirm it. How we arrive at self-expression, and how freedom and choice result in a positive form of self-expression, depend on our motivation to feel alive, or aroused.

Arousal (feeling alive)

Are we naturally motivated to search out leisure? Is leisure one of our basic human drives? The ambiguity surrounding what leisure is makes it difficult to answer this question. But to the extent that leisure is about arousal—about feeling really alive—it is likely that we are fundamentally motivated to pursue it. Many recreation, leisure and travel activities are designed to make us feel alive and aroused. Touring the great cathedrals of Europe, sky-diving, running, even creating a delicacy in the kitchen—these are all activities that can make us feel really alive. It's not the activity we're looking for as much as the feeling of arousal and engagement that results.

Leisure researchers have described arousal as being strongly linked to leisure. In 1990, Thomas Goodale, a leading leisure sociologist, reinforced the "feeling alive" aspect of leisure when he cited Stuart Clause's earlier ideas. Stuart Clause noted he was really alive only about one quarter of the time. Feeling alive for Clause involved states of "creating something, laughter, sorrow, art, and being in the mountains." The sense of *not* being alive, for Clause, included states of "monotony, drudgery, and attending social functions."

When do you feel alive, really alive? What do you feel? Excitement? Joy? Danger? Peace? Sorrow? What situation is most likely to make you feel alive? Is it the birth of a child? An important presentation or exam? A walk in the mountains or by a lake? The solitude of a long run? The first time up on water skis? Returning to school later in life? Or gambling at a blackjack table? The sense of arousal is, like leisure, highly individual and dynamic over time.

Do we really climb mountains because they are there? It is more likely that the motivation to climb Mount Everest is a basic need for arousal and self-expression. We look for experiences that affirm our existence and self-image. Researchers have confirmed that a major component of risk motivation is the need to feel alive—the ultimate form of self-expression. Contrary to popular impressions, high-risk adventurers do not have a death wish. They have a very strong *life* wish.

Climbing Mount Everest is not, thankfully, the only way to get that sense of feeling alive. Everyday activities such as laughter and creating something can provide a similar outcome. In the end, whether it is through sky-diving, the feeling of being lost in a great novel, or cruising down the highway on a motorcycle, the consensus is that we are driven to seek an optimal level of arousal, given who we are.

We each have our own optimal level of arousal, optimal meaning neither too much nor too little. The Optimal Level of Arousal model of human motivation claims that we are driven to seek and achieve this optimal level of arousal. If we experience too much arousal, we begin to feel stress and anxiety, and when there is too little arousal, we feel stress in the form of boredom. Think of a young child of five or six who has outgrown the merry-go-round's excitement, yet for whom the double-loop roller coaster is still too frightening to be fun. It is the mid-range ride that will provide this child with his optimal level of excitement or arousal. If you are a parent, you know that once the child finds that one ride, she can ride it all day. States that bring about optimal arousal may be found in everyday experiences, as well as in rare and important circumstances such as your wedding day. Optimal arousal explains a large part of our motivation to seek leisure. How do we actually get to this state of optimal arousal?

Go with the Flow

Finding the optimal state of arousal has been described as flow, or peak flow, by Mihaly Csikszentmihalyi (in his book entitled *Flow*, 1990), perhaps the best-known researcher in the area of human motivation, creativity, and leisure. Flow occurs when we are so immersed in a moment that we experience an intense awareness of the environment, an autopilot-like guidance of our actions takes over, and at the same time we block out any unrelated thoughts and concerns. High-level athletes and performers sometimes use the phrase "being in the zone" to describe their most intense experiences: a baseball player at bat, a concert pianist mid-performance, or an extreme skier descending the vertical face of a mountain. Flow combines the concept of individual ability with the search for arousal: it is a high-level fit between our ability and the situation we find ourselves in. Like optimal level of arousal, flow is prevented when the situation is too much for our ability and we feel stress, anxiety and fear, or when the situation lacks challenge and boredom ensues. Flow is not limited to risk recreation: it can be achieved in any realm of life, whether it is social, professional, recreation, travel or education. Being in the flow means being entirely lost in the moment, in perfect harmony with an activity, a perfect balance of challenge and ability. Flow results in intense awareness of one's environment or activity, autopilot-like guidance of actions, and an absence of unrelated thought, resulting in immense satisfaction.

In *Surfing the Himalayas,* Fredrick Lenz used a snowboarding metaphor to explain the basic principles of Buddhism. The Buddhist teacher reaches his young American student, a snowboarder, by drawing parallels between the experience of extreme snowboarding down a mountain of fresh powder and the Buddhist concept of mindfulness. In the act of extreme snowboarding, the student must fully immerse himself in the moment, as there is no time to consciously think about the next move once he's riding down the near-vertical slopes. His movements must come instinctively and with no distraction from unrelated thoughts. Essentially he must, and does, become one with the mountain, and while he is snowboarding he experiences mindfulness or flow. Once he stops, even to catch his breath, the state of flow is broken and then he can analyze the last few turns and plan his next moves. This is not possible while he's actually snowboarding because it's a different zone, or different state of consciousness.

Mindfulness is an essential element of flow, as I believe it is of any true leisure experience. For decades, the flow concept has been used to shed light on risk recreation motivation and creativity. Though snowboarding down a pristine Himalayan mountain may be a simple—albeit extreme—example, flow can also occur in everyday living.

Choose Your Stress

Positive stress—of the type required for optimal arousal—can be a crucial element of a successful leisure experience. It is positive stress that makes us feel alive, aware and even invincible at times. Positive stress is like the "just do it" adrenalin-filled stress made popular by Nike and its swoosh. But it does not have to take the form of pushing oneself to the limit in terms of physical skill and ability. It can occur in all areas of life. If we suffer from under-stimulation and lack of challenge, some positive stress to re-engage us with life is clearly needed. Even in terms of a non-physical activity such as reading, full satisfaction will require that the reading material is not too far below our abilities. Leisure requires that we position ourselves between two types of stress: the boredom caused by too little stimulation and the anxiety caused by too much. Somewhere in between boredom and anxiety lies the positive stress related to flow and arousal.

If there is positive stress that makes us feel alive, there is also negative stress that paralyzes our drive and clouds our ambition. While positive stress make real leisure possible, negative stress will surely kill it. Stress is a critical element of leisure in that negative stress can kill leisure drive. We've heard the message that "stress kills" for years now, with proven links between high stress and heart disease. As we have seen, one of the most common misconceptions about free time is that it is inherently enjoyable, satisfying and stress-free. For any situation to be personally rewarding (including free time) it needs to be free of negative stress that prevents us from being fully present in the moment. It's hard, if not impossible, to free up our minds to allow for a flow-like state when we are preoccupied by negative stress. Stress avoidance is a prerequisite for the leisure experience.

We need not look far to find examples of how stress interferes with leisure. Think of the person who brings her work worries home, or home worries to work, and then struggles to unwind or concentrate with a faraway look in her eyes. Think of the athlete who is not performing well because his mind is not on his game, or of the difficulty of getting into a moment of play with the kids after you've done the monthly finances and discovered that the books don't balance. The best way to ruin a good holiday or a day's outing is by being preoccupied with worries over how you will pay for the activity. Preoccupation with limited financial resources can prevent people from taking advantage of leisure opportunities, even if the opportunities are themselves free. Preoccupation and worry prevent leisure, as in the case of new parents desperately trying to enjoy their first night out at the movies with their cellphone turned on in case the babysitter calls.

The good news is that while full engagement in an activity can be initially prevented by virtue of feeling negative stress, the activity itself may soon provide some relief. Strenuous exercise, for example, is considered to be an excellent stress reliever, largely because when we do strenuous exercise, it forces us to focus on the activity and block out other thoughts, even stressful ones.

Essentially we must learn to distinguish between the types of stress that paralyze us and the types that motivate us, in our searching to find positive stress (challenge) and avoid negative stress.

Requirements for Daily Leisure

What do we need in order to experience leisure daily? The specific requirements for daily leisure are simple: self-image, the right balance of stress and an ability to pursue the right types of experiences.

Having a clear self-image is the first and most basic requirement for the leisure experience as our self-image helps us determine what is positive self-expression. A clear and well-defined self-image guides us to pursue those experiences that reinforce it. Without a positive self-image, there is little hope for a leisure experience because our behaviors lack personal meaning and relevance.

It's important to remember that our self-image changes over time, and so do our motivations to pursue various behaviors. For example, when you're young, it's more common to think of yourself as an outdoor risk-taker, but as you get older that may evolve into an image of someone who is connected with nature without needing the risk. So the behavior may change from whitewater rafting to bird watching or gardening. Nothing changes one's self-image like having children; most of us who are parents can point to the time when we became parents as a time when our self-image radically changed, from self-centered party animal, perfect housekeeper, night owl or any number of other individual images, to "parent." Without a solid self-image, we are like a ship drifting at sea, and all that we do—recreation, travel, work, education, family life—is without meaning.

A lack of positive stress or an overabundance of negative stress prevents us from living in the moment and achieving our full capacity. In particular, managing day-to-day stress is essential to being able to experience leisure. But there is more to being able to experience leisure than just stress management. We have to have *ability*—specifically leisure ability. This is the ability to pursue those experiences that reinforce our self-image. Ability to pursue might mean having the right skill level to do what you want, or being able to find the right partners or teammates if they are needed. It could mean overcoming a lack of time or money to pursue your experience, or finding the opportunities for self-expression. Until now, our discussion has been about how we experience leisure from an internal point of view (the deeply personal side of experiencing leisure as a moment of positive self-expression. But our ability to experience includes both internal and external factors. We live in a world where economic, social, work and other factors influence how we feel, what we think and what we do. We can't ignore these external factors when we consider our everyday leisure.

Chapter References

Bregha, Francis J. 1991. "Leisure and Freedom Re-examined." In *Recreation and Leisure: Issues in an Era of Change*. State College, PA: Venture Publishing Inc.

Csikszentmihalyi, Mihaly. 1990. *Flow: The Psychology of Optimal Experience*. New York: Harper Perennial.

Goodale, Thomas L. 1991. "Is There Enough Time?" In *Recreation and Leisure: Issues in an Era of Change*. State College, PA: Venture Publishing Inc.

Iso-Ahola, Seppo E. 1989. "Motivation for Leisure." *In Understanding Leisure and Recreation: Mapping the Past, Charting the Future*. State College, PA: Venture Publishing Inc.

Kelly, John R. 1987. *Freedom to Be*. New York: Macmillan

Lenz, Frederick. 1997. *Surfing The Himalyas: A Spiritual Adventure*. New York: St. Martin's Griffin.

Popcorn, Faith. 1991. *The Popcorn Report.* New York: Doubleday.

Westland, Cor. 1990. "Leisure in an Emerging Community." *World Leisure and Recreation,* World Leisure and Recreation Association. Vol. 32, No. 1 (Spring).

• Chapter 4 •

Leisure Ability

This chapter is about *leisure ability*, which refers to the likelihood that we will experience leisure. Leisure ability depends on several external factors as well as the internal ones discussed in the previous chapter. Some of these help and others hinder leisure ability; some are easy to recognize and others are much subtler. In both cases, awareness of external factors and the ways in which they interact with internal ones is essential to rediscovering leisure.

Leisure Barriers

The best starting point for our discussion of leisure ability is with leisure barriers, which can be thought of as immovable "walls" that prevent us from experiencing leisure. We have seen that stress and an inadequately formed self-image can be barriers to experiencing leisure, but there are other, more concrete barriers as well. We tend to give leisure barriers little attention, except in those moments when we are facing one. We tend to think about barriers when we have missed a family outing because of extra work at the office, or when we put off starting a new activity because of costs or lack of time to really get involved, or when a heavy rain begins just as we are about to set out on our walk. The times we think we have no choice but to say no are the times when we are most aware of our leisure barriers.

Researchers have been studying leisure barriers for decades because marketers in the recreation and tourism industries want to know what factors hinder our involvement in their activities. It makes sense for different sectors of the leisure industry to study barriers to leisure participation, as their success depends on our leisure ability. Libraries could be filled with studies that have included survey questions such as "Please indicate the reason(s) why you do not participate more often in your preferred leisure activities" and "Please indicate your reasons for not taking up new leisure activities." Understanding the things that prevent us from participating more often, if at all, in our leisure activities is extremely valuable information.

Leisure barrier research is important to others on two levels. First, it helps those involved in product development and promotion to better understand leisure activity patterns. Second, governments and academics want to understand our long-term activity patterns; this information is often used when governments introduce new programs, such as health and wellness promotion campaigns. What I have always found interesting about the typical barrier research is that it assumes we want to participate in whatever the leisure activity is and that if we don't participate, it is due entirely to some external barrier. This assumption is important to note because it ignores the fact that we make choices based on our own values and self-image. Sometimes we don't participate in certain activities because we simply don't want to—they don't support our self-image.

The numerous surveys that have been conducted to clarify leisure barriers have produced remarkably consistent results. Consider for a moment how you would respond to some typical leisure barrier research questions:

a) Do you currently plan to take a vacation in the next 12 months? yes or no.
b) If no, why not?
c) Do you currently attend the ballet? yes or no.
d) If no, why not?
e) Do you currently exercise at a club or fitness center? Yes or no.
f) If no, why not?

Ask yourself these questions substituting in any activity that you like to do. To the "if no, why not?" questions, your answer likely included "not enough time" and "not enough money." Lack of time and money are the most common and predictable responses to questions about leisure barriers. This makes sense, given that most of us are time-stressed, and few of us have enough money to do all of the things we would like to do. Furthermore, those who have the money often do not have the time and those who have time often do not have the money.

The popular acceptance of lack of time and money as principal leisure barriers has had an important influence on the leisure industry for decades. And what drives the industry ultimately determines what types of leisure opportunities are available to us. For example, the lack of money response has had a profound impact on the development of leisure products (that is, leisure-related programs, services, vacations and equipment) which are either priced as inexpensively as possible for those who don't have enough money, or priced so high that they come to symbolize prosperity and wealth. Likewise, government leisure services are often subsidized or free of charge in accordance with their goal of financial accessibility.

The lack of time response has prompted the rise of the breakaway package vacation—a shorter, three-to-four-day holiday replacing the traditional two-week family road trip to see the Rocky Mountains or the east coast relatives. The leisure industry has also responded with everything from late-night fitness classes to intense one-day interest courses, recognizing that people are unable and/or unwilling to commit to larger blocks of time. While the industry has been busy responding to time and money barriers, a Canadian geography professor has been busy spearheading a very different approach to leisure barriers.

Leisure Constraints

Ed Jackson from the University of Alberta in Canada has approached leisure barriers with a distinct difference. His key premise is that leisure barriers are not really barriers at all, because a barrier implies some sort of immovable object. In fact, the factors that impede our leisure should be called constraints because, he concluded, they are constantly being negotiated. The leisure constraint approach recognizes the important interaction between internal and external factors in determining leisure ability.

Jackson believes that each one of us is constantly negotiating our leisure constraints, based on what is and what is not important to us as an individual. Time and money are seldom absolute barriers: if something is very important to us, we can and will negotiate to make time, or reprioritize finances accordingly. Negotiating our circumstances is based on our values and self-image.

There are essentially three levels of leisure constraints. In order of importance, these are *intrapersonal*, *interpersonal* and *structural* constraints.

Intrapersonal constraints

The intrapersonal (within the person) level of constraint, what I would call the value-driven level, is based on the assumption that, within reason, we will negotiate apparent barriers to do what we strongly wish to do. In other words, where there's a will, there's a way. For example, when explaining this concept to my university students, I often run a quick experiment. I ask how many in the class consider themselves to be seriously financially constrained—enough to occasionally worry about being able to pay the rent and buy groceries. Usually about two-thirds of the class raise their hands. I then ask, of those who are financially constrained, how many have recently spent a day skiing or snowboarding or an evening out at a club with friends. Many of the same hands will again rise. I then ask how this could be so: As adults who have barely enough money to live, how can they justify spending perhaps a hundred dollars on a day at the ski hill, or an evening in a nightclub? At this point I get a blank, puzzled look, followed by a uniform response of "because I really wanted to go." The thought process for these students (and each one of us) involves negotiation: in this case, the students will accept a diet of macaroni and cheese in order to be able to finance a highly valued experience. Everyone who goes running or works out at the gym during his or her lunch hour has negotiated time (a busy schedule and personal priorities), based on values. They have *made* time to pursue their leisure activities.

Intrapersonal leisure constraints recognize that barriers are not entirely external, and are not absolute. Though time and money constraints may be real and non-negotiable in some cases, in most situations we can negotiate these if we value the leisure experience enough. Most parents constantly juggle income and debt-load with opportunities that they feel are important for their children, such as hockey, little league baseball, dance or family travel.

A good example of this type of leisure negotiation is being witnessed in the trend toward downscaling identified by Faith Popcorn in the early 1990s. Downscaling refers to negotiating a simpler, less hurried lifestyle. Obviously, we have to make some important trade-offs to achieve this. For instance, we may have to take a job that gives us less pay in return for less work (and more free time), or a job that pays less but offers more flexibility and creativity. This is how some people negotiate their lives, choosing to have less material wealth in return for a simpler and calmer way of life. It is not a choice that works for everyone—another illustration of the interaction of individual internal and external factors in producing our leisure ability.

Interpersonal constraints

Interpersonal (between people) constraints are concerned with other people in our lives and the ways in which they affect our leisure ability. For example, a great coach may be the deciding factor in a child's desire to stay involved in a certain sport, perhaps eventually reaching an elite level. Likewise, a poorly trained and critical coach may cause a child to quit even if he or she shows promise and enjoys the activity. Childhood piano teachers are known to be a powerful influence in shaping the careers of successful musicians. Whether we wind up enjoying a family outing has a lot to do with the other members of our family and how we all interact. Whether you play golf or tennis tomorrow has a lot to do with finding someone available to play with. Countless activities depend heavily on the presence and encouragement of others.

In a recent study I conducted for a municipal swimming pool system, I had the pleasure of interviewing four elderly women who, three mornings per week, catch between two and four buses to attend a 6:30 a.m. early-bird swim together. Individually, each woman lives closer to a different pool, but each said she would not swim if it were not for the company of the other three. It's hard to deny that the people around us have a profound impact on our leisure ability.

Structural constraints

The structural level of leisure constraints includes factors that have traditionally been considered leisure barriers: financial capability, work and family commitments, transportation, skill level and the range of leisure choices available. These are the typical time-based reasons people give for not participating in leisure activities. Structural constraints can be real impediments to leisure, but as I have argued in this section, they do not carry the weight of our values and self-image or the influence of those around us. Structural constraints will always be present, but if our desire is strong enough, we can generally negotiate through them. Our redefinition of leisure involves developing an awareness of these factors and recognizing how they unnecessarily limit our leisure ability.

Internal and External Factors

The concept of leisure constraints addresses the push-pull aspect of leisure. Internal motives drive us to search for outlets for positive self-expression to a desired level. At the same time, many other variables such as stress, personal values, people around us, and the structural factors we have just seen need to fall into place in order for us to actually experience leisure. We have begun to view leisure as a subjective experience of mindful positive self-expression. Yet many things that seem to fall outside of our control (external factors) are also important in determining our leisure ability.

Consider someone who is dead set on becoming wealthy. It is understood that in order to get rich this person needs personal ability, desire and entrepreneurship. This person will have to be intelligent, astute and a risk-taker. Success will depend on all of these internal factors, as well as several external ones. External factors for this person may include business partnerships and alliances, industry price fluctuations, secure distribution channels. Other important external factors are removed from the individual's control, such as new technologies, economic up-swings or downturns, globalization and economic policy. Although this person's internal attributes are essential, they will not lead to success unless the right external environment exists as well. Both internal and external factors similarly affect our ability to succeed in our pursuit of leisure.

External factors are not always obvious. For example, technological innovations have had a huge impact on how we travel, to the point where we simply assume we can jet around the globe at will. Without question, our leisure choices and opportunities are influenced by the industry that offers them. By offering us leisure opportunities, the industry is also controlling, or at least setting the parameters on our choices. Do you ever wonder what we are *not* offered? By developing and promoting specific leisure products and services, the industry is coercing us to focus on these as our best choices. The leisure industry both enhances and limits our leisure choices.

For example, when you decide you want to travel, how much does the tourism industry influence your choice of destination? Is it an appealing image you see on a billboard that sways you? A brochure from a well-stocked travel agency's shelf? Have you ever selected a destination that you had never really thought about visiting, but found it so well packaged and promoted that it became the obvious choice? In these situations, we have to ask, "Is the destination a reflection of the traveler's true desire (an act of genuine self-expression) or a convenient, industry-guided alternative with significant appeal?" Are we tricked into thinking that the latest off-the-shelf travel purchase is our true desire when in fact the powerful marketing influence of industry is guiding our choice?

Changes in Travel Opportunities

To illustrate the important role that external and industry factors play, let's examine traveling for pleasure, a leisure experience that most of us can relate to. We take for granted the relative ease with which we can travel for a holiday, to visit family or to conduct business. Our individual motivation or desire to travel is an internal factor, and the desire to travel has remained constant for centuries. But travel has increased dramatically among North Americans over the past few decades.

In the early 1900s, immigrants traveled to North America by steamship which, at the time, was marveled at for its ability to transport huge numbers of people and adhere to a schedule. Prior sailing vessels had relied on unpredictable wind power. The newly built railroad provided access across the continent, where breath-taking landscapes of the rugged and wide-open land quickly became a tourist attraction of global proportion. By the late 1920s the steam train, and later the automobile, allowed people to gain access to areas of the world previously not accessible without considerable hardship—thus creating leisure opportunities. For instance, the average train passenger heading west for a stay at the newly opened Banff Springs Hotel in the glorious Canadian Rocky Mountains would not have even considered the same trip (by horse-drawn coach) only a few years earlier.

The depression of the 1930s shifted the population's priorities away from leisure and onto survival, therefore making travel and tourism a dispensable luxury. While pleasure travel decreased, the awareness of new destinations increased as many men continued to travel the rails in search of work. This helped set up the future of pleasure travel and tourism, once the economy resumed a healthy state.

During World War II, many troops traveled overseas to face battle, and those who returned brought with them a new understanding of the world and a growing acceptance of the ease of travel. The military also was responsible for the greatest travel innovation of our time: the wide-body jet aircraft, used during the war to transport large numbers of soldiers efficiently. Jet aircraft revolutionized travel within a decade. Through fast and convenient air travel, the global village concept was born. Planes opened up the far corners of the globe to curious travelers.

As the 20th century progressed, travel became a real possibility for the average person. While technology was racing ahead, the 20th century was also witnessing unsurpassed economic growth, creating a mass middle class that could afford an automobile and a standard two-week holiday. The automobile, the two-week holiday and jet aircraft represent the greatest developments in pleasure travel in North American history. Automobile tourism quickly grew to exceed all other forms of tourism combined. Road infrastructure, roadside attractions, destination attractions and accommodations also expanded rapidly to meet the resulting demand. Automobile tourism gave rise to mass travel destination centers such as Niagara Falls and Disneyland.

Additional external factors affect our propensity to travel. For example, the value of the dollar has substantial impact on travel habits. When the value of our domestic currency is high in relation to other currencies, we tend to travel abroad; when it is low, we are more likely to travel within our own country or stay at home. The impact currency values have on travel decisions reflects the negotiation that takes place between external factors and internal motivation.

Political climate too can have dramatic impact on our propensity to travel. The same media machine that promotes and facilitates travel throughout the world also provides sobering news reports of violence against tourists throughout the globe. Tourist-directed violence in some developing countries prevents many Ecotourism destinations from becoming the choice of most travelers. On the other hand, highly packaged and secure travel options such as cruise ship travel and all-inclusive gated resorts such as Club Med appeal to those of us who prefer to seek out a safe and confined travel experience. Throughout the 20th century, North Americans have negotiated their desire to travel within the gamut of external factors that have affected travel accessibility.

External factors have similar effects on all the different forms of leisure that we experience. Socio-economic trends present challenges and opportunities in every facet of life. By becoming aware of these factors, we can better negotiate the impact they have on our leisure ability.

In the next section, we will explore the role and impact six external factors have on our leisure. These external factors include economics, work, education, safety and security, government and technology. Each one of these has an influence—often surprisingly—on our ability to experience leisure.

Chapter References

Christie Mill, Robert, and Morrison, Alastair M. 1985. *The Tourism System*. Englewood Cliffs, New Jersey: Prentice-Hall Inc.

Jackson, Edgar L.; Crawford, Duane W.; and Godbey, Geoffery. 1993. "Negotiation of Leisure Constraints." *Leisure Sciences*, Vol. 15.

Krotz, Larry, 1996. *Tourists: How Our Fastest Growing Industry Is Changing the World.* Winchester, MA: Faber and Faber Inc.

Samdahl, Diane M., and Jekubovich, Nancy J. 1997. "A Critique of Leisure Constraints: Comparative Analysis and Understandings." *Journal of Leisure Research*, Vol. 29, No. 4.

Sonnez, Sevil F.; Yiorgos, Apostolopoulos; and Tarlow, Peter. 1999. "Tourism in Crisis: Managing the Effects of Terrorism." *Journal of Travel Research.* Vol. 38, August, pp.13–18.

• Section Two •

Social Trends Affecting Leisure

• Chapter 5 •

Money Matters

In Section One we learned that the ability to experience leisure requires that we understand the deeply internal and personal nature of the leisure experience, as well as the interaction of these internal factors with external ones. One of the most important external factors affecting our ability to rediscover leisure is money.

Money is an incredibly important element of the world in which we live. The multinational corporations and the global economy influence everything from the goods and services available to us, to public policy in virtually all areas of our lives. Globalization means that individual workers—blue-collar or white—have become more detached and removed from their customers, suppliers, distributors, partners and competitors. In the global economy, decisions impacting our way of life are often made in a boardroom far away.

Money is no less important on an individual level, where it is at the root of most of our important life decisions, in areas including education, career, lifestyle, migration and family. Money is often at the heart of what we worry about, and what we argue about. It influences what we aspire to become and what we are willing to endure. Economic values are some of the first values we teach our children and we treat economic responsibility as sign of maturity. Any way we look at it, money matters. But how does money relate to leisure specifically?

Leisure and Economics

The term "leisured class" was coined by the economist Veblen at the turn of the century and referred to those people who were rich enough that they did not have to work. More important than the time that was available was the fact that, unlike the majority of the population, the leisured class was free from day-to-day financial stress. Do the rich really have more leisure? At one level, it is easy to see that they do. Flip through a glossy travel magazine and you will see advertisements for ocean-side villas that most of us will never visit in real life. It is easy to come to the conclusion that more money equals more leisure and less money equals less leisure. But the relationship between money and leisure is more complicated than this.

Money alone cannot buy deeply meaningful personal experiences, whether they be happiness, or love, or leisure. We all know people who work 14-hour days just to be able to retire early, sacrificing leisure, freedom and personal relationships for potential long-term wealth. Likewise, knowing ourselves well enough to pursue positive self-expression, and being able to truly live in and experience the moment, are not necessarily directly associated with money.

It's true that the poor or working poor do not have much money, if any, to spend on what we think of as leisure. In truth, they are mostly at a disadvantage (compared to the rich) in consumer-based leisure. You won't find the poor at those glorious ocean-side villas (unless they are bringing you the towels) but you might find them on the nearby beach. You won't find them staying in a $3,000-a-night room at a Whistler ski resort but you will find them at the campground in Whistler, and probably on the same hiking trails. That's because the biggest difference between the leisure of the rich and the leisure of the poor is *style,* not necessarily content. The difference has less to do with what the two groups are doing and more to do with how they are doing it.

While in university, I took a winter off from my studies to live and work in Banff, Alberta. As a poor student with no family money to draw upon, I had a lifestyle in Banff that was shared with many others of my age and rank. We lived with several people in a crowded one-room cabin and subsisted on a couple of dollars a day. It was a time of economic prosperity; menial jobs were easy to come by, and easy to give up. Most of us worked 16-hour days washing dishes or waiting on tables for several consecutive days, after which we quit the job, and spent several consecutive days skiing and climbing. When the cash ran out, we started over again with another job. Free time during a work period was often spent at the library, because it was free. Clear priorities prevented us from spending any money on expensive social activities in town. All the while the town was fueled by the disposable income of the well-to-do. They stayed in beautiful hotels while we stayed in a one-room cabin; they ate gourmet meals while we ate fifty-cent sausage rolls; they skied in style while we skied with black-market lift passes; they drove a Mercedes to the hill while we hitchhiked—and sometimes caught a ride with them. At the end of the winter we had both experienced Banff, we had both skied the same mountains, but we did these in starkly different styles—living proof of Eric Beck's often cited quote: "At either end of the socio-economic spectrum there lies a leisured class."

Looking back on this experience, many years later, I see that money did not prevent us from experiencing leisure. Indeed, from the perspective of my current age and improved financial situation, I suspect that the leisure I experienced at that time was the most genuine of my life. We were young, healthy, and shared a sense that we were immortal and that our whole lives were ahead of us. Anything was possible. Combine this with the absence of concern over careers, marriages, children or ailing parents, and it is clear that, while poor, we were able to live in the moment, and engage in positive self-expression in a way that few us—with our comparative financial well-being—can access today. Money does not equal leisure. Money is neither necessary to experiencing real leisure, nor is money alone sufficient to produce it.

The Important Connection: Freedom

It is clear that an individual's financial status does not automatically prevent leisure, nor does it guarantee that one will experience true leisure. However, the two are related in important and fundamental ways. Leisure requires a sense of freedom, and, right or wrong, we all associate money with freedom. Money is often seen as the fastest route to achieving full capacity and self-expression. Years ago, a high school guidance counselor asked me, "what would you do if you had a million dollars?" The answer to that question was supposed to make me discover my true inner ambitions, unclouded by the reality of financial constraint. Would a million dollars allow me the freedom to become an artist, doctor, forest ranger or writer? My guidance counselor realized that stress and preoccupation with money was likely to influence even the career choices of a young high school student. Lotteries and financial institutions advertise in terms of freedom—freedom to pursue our dreams, retire early, and open up our dream business (perhaps a fishing lodge up north). For most of us, having money means *freedom from* the financial stress that limits our time, our activities and our ability to live in the moment. Having money also means *freedom to* engage in the kinds of activities that we love, and activities that support our self-image.

The Financial Challenge

Wages form the largest contributions to the income of the majority of North American households. Real wages—wages adjusted to inflation— also are directly related to our standard of living. In recent years the income of most households has gone up slightly but *not* because we're making that much more money; it's because households have more people earning a wage.

Since the 1920s we have seen major swings in the growth of real wages. From 1920 to the mid-1930s real wages grew slowly, about 10 percent each decade. From the 1940s to the end of the 1960s, it grew about 37 to 45 percent throughout each of the three decades. From 1970 to 1995, the average real wage has grown about 32 percent in total—less than it did in the one decade of the 1960s. Disposable income has generally stagnated for the past 25 years as a higher cost of living and higher taxes have offset increases in wages.

Stress over money is not just about how little money we earn but also about the stress of how much money we may owe, or debt burden. So it's not surprising that young people just coming out of college or university and in the process of establishing a home and family tend to have the highest debt burdens relative to earning ability. Unfortunately, this stress is added to the stress of paying off student loans and starting a career, often in a new city with little or no support from family and friends. These forms of stress can have a substantial impact on leisure ability. This is the type of stress that can turn the monthly balancing of the books into an argument, or make going out for dinner unthinkable. For many of us, money-stress can still push us to work more, or make us feel guilty over the smallest discretionary expenditure. The "no matter how hard I try I just can't seem to get ahead" mentality lingers, hindering our leisure ability and taking the freedom out of free time.

Global and local economic trends directly affect our individual financial situations, and thus our ability to experience leisure. The truth is, we are getting ahead financially. Since the early 1990s, our economic situation has improved. In North America virtually all economic indicators have risen, pointing to improved economic conditions. Yet despite the improved economic conditions of recent years, we all recognize that boom-and-bust cycles are shorter, and that financial uncertainty is always just around the corner. When times are bad, we have to work extremely hard just to survive, and hopefully not to lose what we have gained. When times are good, we have to work even harder, to take advantage of the opportunity to build some security for the uncertain future. Concerns over the environment have led us to be acutely aware that we are living on a small and finite planet. More and more of us are competing for a slice of a pie that is perceived to be shrinking. The result is a scarcity mentality that directly impacts our ability to find leisure.

The scarcity mentality occurs when we feel we have to get as much as we can now because we have little confidence that resources will be available in the future. Imagine being seated at a dinner table with your family of several large older brothers. As the plate of chicken is being passed around, you realize that once that plate leaves your hands it's going into the hands of your older brothers who will easily devour everything on the plate. As you are still holding the plate, you decide to take an extra piece or even two, though you are not necessarily that hungry. You take the extra chicken because you don't have any confidence in that plate of chicken coming around a second time. This is, in essence, a scarcity mentality. A scarcity mentality in a boom-and-bust economy can bring about a preoccupation with making as much as we can now. This drive can be so powerful that it prevents us from living in the moment and thus experiencing leisure.

The perception that no matter how hard we try, we may not be able to achieve our financial and lifestyle goals is not just about scarcity. It involves a sense of losing control over our financial well-being. Few argue against the efficiencies and power of the global economy. Nor can it be denied that a new wave of entrepreneurial millionaires has been born out of globalization. But there has been another impact for the millions of workers who are subject to its policies and business practices. Globalization has resulted in a new economy where the ubiquitous financial markets rule, and most of us have little access to the decision-making. Communities and workers are far removed from the decision-making process that impacts—for better or worse—our individual lives and communities.

How important is control? Being at the whim of a global economy appears to be more and more of a worry. In 1999, the World Trade Organization was rudely awakened to this concern when protesters crippled their annual meeting in Seattle, Washington. Among the issues being protested was the loss of control over economic decision-making at the local level. The Seattle meetings were a glimpse into the groundswell of frustration that is beginning to surface. Less control over our financial well-being adds to the overall stress of living in our age. It adds to the stress of reading the morning newspaper and realizing that a downturn across the globe will affect the stability of our local economy and standard of living.

The Impact of Economic Uncertainty

The consistent economic growth of the 1940s to the 1960s produced a sense of stability that has not been matched since, nor does it appear it will return in the near future. Though the 1990s were good to most North Americans, they were also fickle and thus somewhat stressful. Most of us are working more, not less, and we still have an ever-widening gap between economic classes in our society.

The fact that many of us will always struggle with money and many of us will never have as much money as we think we want or need has, in general, a negative impact on our leisure ability. Keeping up with the Joneses will fill our garages full of stuff, but this seldom brings about the experience of living in a moment of positive self-expression. The modest financial gains that we've realized in the past decade have generally come at a cost of personal stress and social change that makes money more of an obstacle to be negotiated then an opportunity to be celebrated. As long as the economy experiences swings, people will continue to stress over their own financial well-being.

Overall, money is an especially important factor to consider in our assessment of leisure ability because it penetrates so deeply into our everyday lives, throughout our entire lives. For us to realize leisure as an experience of living in a moment of positive self-expression, we need to live with minimal stress, including money-related stress. The first step to managing money-related stress in relation to our leisure ability is to understand the role of money in our lives and what, if any, stress it creates for us personally. This understanding will help us negotiate our internal desire for leisure with external money-related developments we will face throughout our lives.

Chapter References

Kelly, John R. 1991. "Leisure Behaviors and Styles: Social, Economic, and Cultural Factors." In *Understanding Leisure and Recreation: Mapping the Past, Charting the Future.* State College, PA: Venture Publishing Inc.

Krakauer, John. 1990. *Eiger Dreams: Ventures among Men and Mountains.* New York: Anchor Books Doubleday (Eric Beck's quote is on page 77).

Neulinger, John. 1991. "Free Time, Economics, and Leisure." *Leisure and Recreation.* World Leisure and Recreation Association, Spring.

Rashid, Abdul. 1993. "Seven Decades of Wage Changes." *Perspectives on Labour and Income.* Statistics Canada, Summer.

Searle, Mark S. and Brayley, Russell E. 1993. *Leisure Services in Canada.* State College, PA: Venture Publishing Inc.

Serena, Arnold. 1991. "The Dilemma of Meaning." In *Recreation and Leisure: Issues in an Era of Change.* State College, PA: Venture Publishing Inc.

• Chapter 6 •

Working Hard at Leisure

Max Weber, the 20th century philosopher, captured in words a question that many of us struggle with every day. Weber asked, "Do we work to live or live to work?" This simple but far-reaching question makes us think about the role of leisure and work in our everyday lives. This question also highlights just how intertwined work and leisure are. It's hard to think about one without the other because they have played off each other for so long as opposites.

Most of us don't have a choice about work—we have to work. That makes work a non-negotiable part of our life as well as a non-negotiable activity within our day. But it doesn't necessarily make it an obvious obstacle to our leisure ability. What determines whether work positively or negatively affects our leisure ability is not so much that we have to work, or even how much we work, but how we view our work. An eight-hour shift at work can feel like a lifetime if you hate what you do or it can fly by if you're one of those people who just love your job. Your work can add to or detract from your quality of life.

Work impacts leisure ability in one of two ways: if work provides us with opportunities for self-expression and a way of achieving our full capacity, then it facilitates our leisure ability. On the other hand, if we see work as something that stifles our self-expression and holds us back from achieving our full capacity, then it detracts from our leisure ability. Work clearly has the potential to impact our leisure ability in both positive and negative ways.

The Day Still Revolves Around Work

Work holds different meanings for different people. On a personal level, our work may be the simplest way to explain who we are *(what you do is who you are)* or the best opportunity for advancement in life *(you can do anything if you work hard)*. Some people, mostly men, associate work with being a provider, much like the hunters and gatherers of the past, except that spears and vast wilderness have been replaced with laptops and cyberspace. We sometimes tell people who act as if they have too much free time to "get a job," while we tell those people who take their job too seriously to "get a life." We sometimes warn students, "just wait until you get out into the real world," to make work sound really important. In any case, we have a tendency to talk about work as the number one criterion of the real world, of being an adult and of being respectable. Even educational institutions are increasingly measured on the employability of their graduates, while I have yet to see anyone providing a report on a leisure ability measure for graduates.

Work, and more specifically jobs, are important indicators of economic performance. The unemployment figure, representing the number of people who want to work but cannot find work, is a measure of economic health. Politicians are re-elected for their track records in job creation. The clout of any particular industry is often a function of the number and quality of jobs it can produce and sustain, as in technology's current situation.

Work represents a dilemma with respect to our leisure ability. On the one hand, it can be a non-negotiable obligation allowing little or no freedom and choice. On the other hand, it's also the cornerstone of hope and aspiration as a means of achieving full capacity and self-expression. Work is an important external factor affecting our leisure ability, and one that virtually all of us must address.

Who Works? And How Much?

Who works and how much depends on the economy. When the economy is strong we find that most of us who can work do, and when the economy slows down more of us are left scrambling to find work. The economy of the 1990s (and into 2000) has been, by and large, very strong, which means most of us are working and some of us are working a lot.

In the 1990s the United States and Canada experienced the lowest unemployment rates in more than two decades. The United States reached an unemployment rate just below 5 percent and Canada's fell below 7 percent. At these levels many analysts say we're at or close to full employment, meaning that there are jobs out there for almost everyone who wants to work.

Over the past century the amount we work has changed as well. We started from very long work weeks in the early part of the 20th century and slowly worked our way down to the standard 40-hour work week by mid-century. The 40-hour work week remained the standard for several decades, although since the 1980s many of us are working more than 40 hours.

The most important present-day change to hit the workforce began in the early 1970s when women joined the workforce *en masse*. In the next 30 years, women doubled, and in some cases quadrupled, their presence in the workforce.

As we enter the new millennium, we find the proportion of self-employed is increasing while the proportion of unionized workers is decreasing. We also find that more and more young people are working, balancing school with a job, and more older people are opting to work longer in life.

What is causing these changes in "who works and how much"? Are we working more because we want to, have to or just because we can? If it's because we want to, does that mean work is no longer that bleak activity that we think of as being opposite to leisure? If it's because we have to, does that mean work is becoming an even bigger obstacle to our leisure?

The Leisure and Work Relationship

It would be simple to describe the relationship between work and leisure in the traditional sense as opposites. But we know that the personal meaning of the activity is more important than the activity itself. To claim that work is the opposite of leisure is to ignore the fact that it can and often does produce many of the same arousal and flow types of outcomes as leisure. This slow integration is witnessed through the growth of various workplace initiatives such as home work, alternative work schedules, increased employee participation, sabbaticals and other job satisfaction measures.

Three work-related trends affecting our leisure ability have emerged in the past several decades, resulting in a changing workplace.

1. The integration of leisure and work

At some point in the latter half of the 20th century, the concept of work evolved into that of a career. This meant a shift from work as exclusively negative toward work as linked to aspirations, with an assumption that at some level most of us want to work. Our expectations also evolved to the point where most of us now expect a fairly high level of satisfaction and self-expression at work. During the 1980s, this was often referred to as empowerment. We recognize and expect that work should be more than a paycheck and that work and leisure should not be opposites.

For the past two decades the academic community has acknowledged that leisure and work are perhaps more alike than they are different. Various researchers have concluded that many of the outcomes we expect from leisure, such as creativity and challenge, are increasingly found in our work. This has led researchers such as Judith Brook of Massey University in New Zealand to conclude, "leisure must be considered as part of the broader domain of work and non-work activities and the relationship between them defined according to the actors' own perceptions."

Robert Stebbins, from the University of Calgary, has drawn a link between serious leisure (a term he coined that refers to leisure as hobbies, amateur-level activity and volunteering) and paid work. Some hobbies such as crafts, painting and even stamp collecting can become a second source of income. Amateurs in various areas such as the arts, photography, music and others can become professionals when they are paid, even at a low rate. Volunteers are sometimes motivated to give their time for work-related reasons such as enhancing their résumés and networking. When these activities result in paid work they offer another link between leisure and work.

As we have moved from thinking of work as drudgery to thinking of work as a satisfying career we have also raised our expectations of work. So job satisfaction survey results are another way for us to check the leisure and work integration. Recent research reported that about nine out of ten of us are satisfied with the work we do, even though we may not always like those we work for. Given that work represents such a large part of our day, the integration of work and leisure means enhanced leisure opportunities for many people.

2. Losing security

We know that stress is the "number one killer" of our leisure ability. Negative stress creates a preoccupation that takes away from our ability to live in the moment. "There are no secure jobs, only secure people" is a statement repeated time and again in the past few decades to describe the new reality of the workplace. Though it's true, we can't forget that the road to becoming a secure person can often be a stressful one. Insecurity with something as important as work can cause us to become so preoccupied that we become ineffective both at work and at home.

It was recently reported that family stress levels were higher in the late 1990s than 50 years ago at the cusp of the post-war era. Unstable and insecure job conditions were among the top three causes of stress. Three out of four people 30 years of age and younger reported job instability as a major source of stress. A 1997 international study of the work patterns of white-collar employees found that the majority of workers were holding off on vacations because of job instability. The same study reported that some people choose to avoid telecommuting for fear of appearing dispensable. Job instability also drives people to work longer, to appear to work longer (by staying late and writing e-mail messages at all hours of the night), and even to take on additional jobs.

In the late 1990s Statistics Canada conducted an interesting study that asked workers which of the following they would prefer:
(a)   work fewer hours for less pay
(b)   work the same hours for the same pay
(c)   work more hours for more pay

Almost two in three workers would like to work the same hours for the same pay (b), but just over 27 percent would prefer to work more hours for more pay (c). What is most revealing about these responses is who makes up the group that would prefer to work more hours for more pay. This group is more likely to be non-unionized than unionized, be non-permanent rather than permanent, have no pensions, and be younger rather than older. The proportion of self-employed is increasing while the proportion of unionized workers is decreasing. Workplace changes of the past two decades, however needed, have resulted in decreased job stability and growing stress that can impede our leisure ability.

3. We're doing well, but doing well is taking more work

By and large we *are* doing well. North Americans enjoy an extremely high standard of living relative to other parts of the world. But for many of us, doing well means more work, resulting in that mouse-on-the-treadmill feeling.

If we are working more because we want to work more, then working might mean more opportunities for leisure. If we're working more because we feel we have no choice, then working more becomes a huge obstacle that detracts from leisure ability. Likewise, if we feel we have to work more just to keep our jobs then this becomes a powerful external factor that takes away from our leisure ability.

Working more for some of us might represent a certain level of importance and status (people who only work a standard work week fail to give the impression that they are on the cutting edge of anything). For others working extra means that something else must be dropped. It means a trade-off whereby one part of the day suffers in favor of another, and the part that suffers could be our child care arrangements, family time, personal fitness, other recreational and educational pursuits or spousal relationships.

A growing number of women must make just such a trade-off after having a child. Over the past several decades, as more and more women have entered the workforce, the amount of time spent away from work after having a baby has steadily decreased because of money, or fear of losing their marketability, or because it gives them the type of balance and satisfaction they're looking for in life.

Balancing the work and non-work parts of life is important for workers and for companies who want to improve worker productivity. Alternative work arrangements have become a common way to address balance, and arguably they are an example of the kind of changes women have brought to the workplace. Alternative work arrangements come in a variety of forms, including telecommuting, job-sharing, flex-time, compressed work weeks, shift work and so on.

The underlying goal of alternative work arrangements is to minimize time stress. It is safe to say that alternative work arrangements offer more flexibility and control over daily scheduling, which usually has a favorable impact on our leisure ability. However, not all types of alternative work arrangements actually reduce the amount of time stress we experience. A recent study on this topic noted that flex-time (whereby workers work a standard work week but they have the flexibility to determine when those hours are worked) was the only arrangement that actually resulted in decreased feelings of time stress.

As a population, we are doing well in terms of our standard of living, but working more to achieve this. Working more is an obstacle to leisure ability when it is involuntary and non-negotiable. The personal benefits of working more for some people may be as real as being able to pay the rent and buy some extra food. For others working more can be no more beneficial than appearing indispensable to the company.

Work without pay

If it looks like work, sounds like work, and feels like work it's probably work, even though it's really volunteering or housework, which is essentially work we don't get paid for. Each year in North America we dedicate over 250 billion hours to unpaid household work, and the amount of time we volunteer is estimated to be over 10 billion hours.

Volunteering can be a valuable leisure expression when it's something we do simply because we want to and it supports our self-image. For example, the retired accountant who devotes 20 hours each week to leading a scout troop, the mechanic who is a Big Brother to a boy, or the figure skating mom who spends four hours driving girls from one lesson to another.

Throughout our hospitals, soup kitchens, food banks and church basements we can find thousands of people each day willingly contributing their time.

However, volunteerism can also be something we do because we feel we should do it, or have to, and that can change the way we view this expenditure of time. For example, a morning spent volunteering in your child's classroom may be a valued experience that reinforces your image of yourself as an attentive parent. Or, if you are told that your child's field trip will be canceled unless three more parent drivers are found by the next day, you may feel obligated to rework your schedule to be one of those drivers.

Are we volunteering by choice or because we feel we have to? Most of us volunteer because we want to and it reinforces our self-image. Over time what has changed is the view of organizations that rely on volunteers. Not-for-profit organizations (which are almost completely driven by volunteers) are designed to fill the social, recreational and managerial needs and wants that other institutions, such as governments, cannot address. For example, we wouldn't have many of the children's sports opportunities, such as baseball, community basketball and so on if it were not for volunteers. Government institutions such as hospitals, schools, and parks and recreation agencies also provide a variety of programs and services that would not be delivered if it were not for volunteers. A growing number of organizations and institutions consider volunteer labor as the basis of their service delivery because they are forced to do more with less. When volunteers make up the shortfall in providing services that we think are very important then volunteerism tends to look more like work, and when we feel obligated to volunteer it becomes very much like work.

By now housework should have been virtually eliminated through the wonders of technology. Indeed, the amount of time spent on housework has decreased. The average amount of time spent on household maintenance was 1,223 hours in 1962, and it dropped to 1,164 in 1992. Housework is no less a concern today than it was 30 years ago (although we have gained 59 hours, just over a weekend of time, away from housework).

We cannot look at housework's impact on leisure ability without looking at gender differences. Since the early 1960s women have decreased household maintenance time by about 10 percent, but in that same time they have more than doubled their participation in the workforce—hence the importance of balance. Men have increased their share of household responsibility by about 5 percent but their presence in the workforce has remained constant.

Meal preparation and related cleaning is still the most time-consuming of our household responsibilities. Women now spend more time on shopping, transportation and volunteering, while men spend more time on repairs, maintenance, meal preparation and care of clothes. Smaller homes have given us some timesaving reductions over the past 30 years, along with fewer detached homes and fewer children per household. Adding to our household demands are eldercare, and more rooms and amenities within our homes to care for. If little else, technology has given us cleaner clothes. The time and energy required per load of laundry has drastically decreased since the days of the wringer-washer but apparently we now wash our clothes more often, thereby eliminating any efficiency gains we've experienced. For most of us, household labor is no less a concern today than it was 35 years ago.

It's the Fit That Counts

The old relationship of leisure and work as opposites has at least begun to fade as more and more people realize that leisure (as self-expression) can often be found just as easily at work as it can at home. This development bodes well for the future of leisure, but work can still be an important obstacle in our search for leisure, as it can create a powerful stress. As long as we live in such a way that work does not complement our self-image, with our work completely separate from who we think we are, work will remain an obstacle to our leisure ability.

Chapter References

Akyeampong, Ernest, B. 1997. "Work Arrangements: 1995 Overview." *Perspectives*. Statistics Canada, Spring.

Brook, Judith A. 1993. "Leisure Meanings and Comparisons with Work." *Leisure Studies*, Vol. 12.

Canadian Centre for Philanthropy. 2000. *National Survey of Giving, Volunteering and Participating.* Toronto: The Centre, February.

Drolet, Marie, and Morissette, Rene. 1997. "Working More? Less? What Do Workers Prefer?" *Perspectives on Labor and Income.* Statistics Canada, Winter.

Earl, Louise. 1999. "Baby Boom Women—Then and Now." *Perspectives on Labor and Income.* Statistics Canada. Vol. 3 (Autumn).

Fast, Janet E., and Frederick, Judith A. 1996. "Working Arrangements and Time Stress." *Canadian Social Trends.* Statistics Canada, Winter.

Jackson, Chris. 1996. "Measuring and Valuing Households' Unpaid Work." *Canadian Social Trends.* Statistics Canada, Autumn.

Marshall, Katherine. 1993. "Dual Earners: Who's Responsible for Housework?" *Canadian Social Trends.* Statistics Canada, Winter.

Monette, Manon. 1996. "Retirement in the 90s: Going Back to Work." *Canadian Social Trends.* Statistics Canada, Autumn.

Noadwodny, Richard. 1996. "Working at Home." *Canadian Social Trends.* Statistics Canada, Spring.

Rashid, Abdul. 1993. "Seven Decades of Wage Changes." *Perspectives.* Statistics Canada, Summer.

Saul, John Ralston. 1995. *The Unconscious Civilization.* Toronto: Anansi. CBC Massey Lectures series. http://www.statcan.ca/english/econoind/indic.htm

Stebbins, Robert. 1998. *After Work: The Search for an Optimal Lifestyle.* Calgary: Detselig Enterprises Ltd.

Weber, Max. 1922. *Economy and Society.* Berkeley: University of California Press.

• Chapter 7 •

I'm Glad It Doesn't Affect Me

"I'm just glad it doesn't affect me" is what we may think when we read about the latest violent robbery, murder or terrorist attack. It's the kind of news that has become background noise for most of us, but the truth is it does affect each one of us in our daily lives and our search for leisure.

According to reported crime, only a small percentage of the population is actually victimized in any one year, but all of us are subject to the fear of crime—the fear of becoming a victim. Arguably, crime's biggest impact on our leisure ability is in our attempts to shield and protect ourselves and the people we love. The way we respond to the threat of crime is the key to understanding how crime impacts our leisure ability.

Indirectly crime limits our choices in obvious and less obvious ways. For instance, many of us choose not to have after-movie drinks at a biker bar or vacation in a war-torn region of the world. There are less obvious effects as well—a middle-aged woman considering an evening class may be deterred by the after-class walk to her car through a darkened parking lot; an elderly couple may decide not to take an evening stroll because of a vague feeling of discomfort; a youth must navigate through his day by observing the unwritten rules of the schoolyard.

Since the 1980s we have generally come to believe that crime has increased, and this perception can give us the feeling that we have lost some of our freedom. Gone are the days when being careful simply meant staying out of a stranger's car (especially if it was a hand-painted cube van driven by crazed hippies). Today the fear of becoming a victim is a part of virtually every area of daily life, including the home, public places, the workplace, schools, roads (road rage), travel destinations and even airline travel (air rage). This fear acts as a constant reminder of our need to be vigilant, defensive and suspicious.

Certainly being more defensive and suspicious of others limits our freedom and everyday choices, but crime and its associated fear affects us in a deeper way as well. It can, over time, shape our idea of what it means to be free. For some people walking the streets at night is something that is not even considered—it's not a part of what you do. Why? Because some of us have been conditioned to see the world in such a way that freedom is quite narrow and guided by the range of defensive behaviors we use to avoid becoming victims of crime.

Has Crime Increased?

Despite what we think about the rate of crime, reported crime has steadily decreased since the early 1990s in both the United States and Canada. Violent crimes such as murder, attempted murder, robbery and youth crime have decreased. On the other hand, crimes such as prostitution, auto-theft and gaming and betting crimes have increased. Overall, there has been no dramatic shift up or down in the crime rate, but the trend has been a modest drop.

Youth crime and gang violence is one area of crime that has managed to capture our attention in recent years. This area too has seen a small reduction in the rate of reported crime; however, the rate of violent crimes has increased compared with other crimes such as property crimes carried out by youth. What experts find most alarming is the rise in violent crimes carried out by girls between 14 and 16 years of age. Girls still have crime rates far below that of boys, but girls' rates are increasing faster than boys'.

Victimization Patterns

The extent to which we change our behaviors to avoid crime is largely based on how likely we think it is that we could become a victim. In the United States, if you are young, black and male you're the most likely target of violent crimes. In fact, teens are more likely to be victims of violent crime than the elderly, and men are more likely to be the target of any violent crime than women, except for rape and sexual assaults.

In Canada, those who live in urban centers have a 27 percent greater chance of being victimized than those who live in rural settings. Women and youth run a greater risk of victimization as well (two-thirds of all victims of youth violence are other youth or children). Three out of four victims of youth violent crime know their assailants. On the other hand, strangers account for about 68 percent of non-sexual assaults and 86 percent of robberies. Victimization still, as in the past, is most likely to happen in a private home which, in part, explains why between 1974 and 1992 (and probably still today) a woman was nine times more likely to be killed by her husband than by a stranger.

Much of what we know about victimization and crime in general depends on how crimes are reported. Here we have some conflicting views on what our crime data are really telling us. Some sociologists warn that we should be careful about how we interpret crime rates today because changes in reporting practices have inflated the statistics and given us the false impression that some types of crimes are increasing. The standard example given is that a typical schoolyard fight of the 1970s was probably not reported as a crime, whereas today's zero tolerance means that even the slightest schoolyard scuffle is often reported as an assault. On the other hand, the National Council for the Prevention of Crime claims that up to 90 percent of sexual assaults and 68 percent of other assaults go unreported. It's hard to know what we should believe when it comes to crime statistics, but we do know that whether we have been personally victimized or not, we're likely to allow the fear of being victimized to affect our behaviors in ways that invariably limit our leisure ability.

What We Think About Crime

A 1997 NBC/*Wall Street Journal* poll reported that 57 percent of Americans believe that crime and education are the two top social issues and that more than half of all Americans are personally afraid of becoming victims of crime. In Canada this figure is supported by a *Maclean's* Magazine poll that indicated 30 percent of Canadians are afraid to walk in their own neighborhood. Most people generally think that violent crime accounts for about 30 percent of all reported crime, although in fact it accounts for no more than 10 percent. It appears that we are convinced crime is getting worse, regardless of what we hear otherwise.

Crime and the fear of victimization have had a big impact on tourism. The Persian Gulf War in 1990 discouraged travel not just within the region but throughout the world. Egypt experienced a 43 percent drop in tourism as a result of terrorist activity in 1992. The tourism industry has learned to treat crime very seriously, for obvious reasons, but it's also important to give this concern a sobering second look. During the mid-1980s, as terrorism was on the rise, 28 million Americans traveled abroad and 162 were either hurt or killed as a result of terrorist activity, resulting in a .00057 percent chance of terrorist victimization. These are not the kind of odds most of us would expect to result in a fear of travel.

Part of what fuels the perception of personal risk is the thought that it can be so random—that any one of us can be a victim at any time. If the media are guilty of contributing to a sense of paranoia, it has been in directly or indirectly implying that victimization is largely random. Though some victimization is random, the majority is not. For example, home invasion assaults and robberies are some of the most bone-chilling crimes and the basis for many headlines. It's generally not until we get to about the third paragraph that we read that the victim and the assailant knew one another. Yet how many people actually read beyond the "home invasion" headline to get the whole story?

The best way for us to survey the real impact crime and the fear of crime have on our leisure ability is to assess some of the more common ways we respond to this threat.

How Have We Responded?

Essentially we have changed the way we think and act to become more suspecting, sheltered and defensive. In so doing we have limited our freedom, our choices and opportunities for self-expression as well.

We can assume that the fear of becoming a victim of crime is a constraint to leisure participation much like other barriers we've discussed, including lack of time and money. Though lack of time and money are the most common top-of-mind constraints, fear of crime is as important, if not more important, as a constraint. Most of us struggle with the question of whether we have enough time or money only after we've considered our safety. If it's not a safe option, we don't care if we have enough time or money because we're not going to do it anyway. A family vacation to Central America or Mexico could be very inexpensive if you stayed off the beaten track, but most of us will wait and save until we can afford to stay at a reputable hotel or resort.

Structuring our children

In the past two decades of the 20th century—roughly coinciding with the increased awareness of crime in the early 1980s—we witnessed a curious change in our children's play and recreation activity. More and more children were enrolled in structured recreation programs (programs that are scheduled and supervised), ranging from day camps in the off-school periods to evening sports, arts and even educational programs. Recreation agencies such as the YMCA, Boys and Girls Clubs and many others have been bursting at the seams. In this same 20-year period we witnessed an enormous growth in the number of new youth recreation organizations. There is no doubt that the demand for children's programs increased in these 20 years.

What is driving this curious change in the way that children play? Have baby boomer parents changed their ideals and decided to embrace the concept of structure? Are children's programs so good that kids are simply flocking to them? Not exactly. Some of this change could be the result of that huge group of baby boomers having their own children (the echo generation, according to David Foot), or the increase in dual-earner families who need year-round day-care, or cuts to school budgets and the elimination of non-core curriculum activities.

But a more complete explanation centers on the dilemma that most parents today face in raising children. On the one hand, children must play and they have to be free to spontaneously explore and learn. On the other hand, common wisdom tells us that parents just can't allow their children to roam free, even in their own neighborhoods, because it is too risky and irresponsible. Jay Teitel provided a lament to play in his 1999 *Saturday Night* article called "The Kidnapping of Play." He states that "the idea of kids running around alone on the streets, through a neighborhood, evokes alarm, even in kids." Most of us who grew up during the 1970s or earlier likely spent our summer days playing throughout every nook and cranny of the neighborhood and seldom came home other than to grab some food. Our parents didn't know where we were playing or what we were doing, but they knew we were somewhere close by and when we got hungry enough we would come home. Kidnappers, pedophiles and other sordid predators (excluding the local 12-year-old bullies outside the corner store) were not a concern back then. So we simply, and naturally, played.

Today the fear of potential harm to our children is overwhelming and, as Teitel points out, the fear is fueled in part by media, like the 1990 magazine headline that read "The Mounting Toll of Missing Children," which emphasized parents' vigilance as the only defense against the growing crime targeted at children. The same article points out that in 1989, 574 children were abducted, all but four by one of the child's parents. The other four were eventually found. Harm has, and does, come to children; it is real. But the question is, have we used a sledgehammer to drive in a tack?

Returning to the dilemma facing parents today, it appears that many of us try to be vigilant and understanding. Today we walk this fine line by signing our kids up for recreation programs that offer a balance between safety and fun.

We have to ask ourselves whether our children have lost out on an opportunity for freedom and self-expression because of our vigilance. Or have children not lost anything because unrestricted neighborhood play, like that many of us experienced, is something they have never known so they don't miss it? Most parents value play opportunities for their children, even though they are in the form of structured play, and even if they mean endless driving and waiting. For most parents this is a negotiated decision based on how much we value leisure and play and how much we fear the world in which we live.

Those who work with our children

For many parents, it is not enough to have their kids enrolled in supervised programs, although it's a good start. Increasingly, parents have turned their attention to who is working with their children in these supervised programs.

For years, we have known that people who prey on children can be as readily found in a doctor's office, school or locker room as in a seedy cube van, but we have been reluctant to believe it can happen anywhere. That is not the case today. The media is filled with reports of child abuse cases involving children's organizations, day camps, churches and sports leagues at all levels. Today, youth and sports organizations of all types must put their staff and volunteers through a rigorous screening process involving police record checks and references. These measures are designed to keep children safe and provide parents with peace of mind.

These screening practices are an indication of how seriously we treat the threat of potential harm to our children. We've basically taken them off the streets and out of the parks and put them into programs, but even then we have gone as far as we can to maintain our vigilance.

Safe schools

School violence has been an issue in North America for decades and our response to this issue has been to impose various measures—some quite radical. Many states are still struggling to improve upon their safety, discipline, alcohol and drugs rating which is used as a benchmark along with other curriculum measures. We've responded to this issue by imposing a variety of measures, including metal detectors, uniformed security officers, video surveillance cameras, school uniforms and mandatory photo identification, all with the goal of making the school a safer place. It is proposed that the threat of violence results in a level of stress that takes away from a student's ability to focus and concentrate on learning, similar to the way stress detracts from our leisure ability.

The safety and security measures we have imposed in our schools reinforce the idea that schools are a place for learning and growth, and anything that interferes with learning and growth must be addressed. No one can argue that schools should not be as safe as possible, but safety measures must not be so imposing that they become a distraction in themselves.

The upside to our vigilance is that we're quite sure that our kids are safer today. The downside to our vigilance is that our kids are likely to have less freedom, choice and natural opportunities for self-expression. It's not that they don't play—they do—but increasingly their play is controlled, guided and at the mercy of parents and other adults. Most often after-school programs involve adult supervision and then kids have to further rely on their parents because of the cost and transportation involved. Unlike the kid of the 1970s or earlier, children today have limited freedom to pick who they play with, when they get together and what they do. This is not to falsely glamorize the memory of the "good old days," because they were not always so good. Rather, it is to illustrate how much things have changed in a short period of time, and to make us think about what might occur in the future.

Living in enclaves

In recent years, technological advances have made home security systems a more accessible and common option. Though the rate of reported household crimes such as break and enters has decreased, the level of concern surrounding household crimes has not lessened. Most of us are satisfied with standard household safety measures (locked doors and windows, barred lower-level windows, safety lighting and so on). However, throughout North America (and in the United States more than Canada) some people are opting for more extreme safety measures such as gated communities.

Gated communities represent the extreme of home security. The gated community is a typical subdivision, most popular with older age groups, that is surrounded by large, impassable walls with security gates designed to keep out people who do not belong. These communities provide a greater sense of security inside the compound but can also create more fear of what is outside the walls.

People will do whatever they think is necessary to protect home and family, even if it means living in a gated community. However, think about what a gated community says about the city it is a part of. It says that crime is perceived as so prevalent that those who can afford it believe they need to live in a walled compound to protect themselves. These communities represent a move toward a more segmented society and, in this case, a physical widening of the gap between the rich and poor or the civil society and the criminals.

Our public parks

We love our parks. Ever since their inception, public parks have faced the challenge of providing recreation opportunities and urban respite for everyone in a way that still allows people to feel safe. Parks such as Central Park in New York City have been the butt of jokes and the source of urban myths as to how likely one is to be robbed, mugged or murdered in the park (the first murder in Central Park took place in 1873). A public park is an example of the relationship between leisure ability and safety. On the one hand, a park is a public place that is supposed to facilitate opportunities for freedom, choice and self-expression, whether in play, quiet reflection or organized sport. On the other hand, if a park is not perceived to be a safe place, it will not facilitate leisure ability. The most common way to make a park safe has been to impose more security, rules and restrictions, which can take away from the park's ability to inspire freedom and expression. A balance between leisure potential and safety is essential. Some people take matters into their own hands and find this balance by restricting their park use to safe periods, and others might go for a walk or run any time, as long as they're holding a leash with a Shepherd-Rottweiler cross at the end and a can of bear spray in the other hand.

In the past several decades parks have changed in design to become safer places. Some of the safety-enhancing measures include increased lighting for nighttime use and planting deciduous trees in place of sight-limiting coniferous trees to increase visibility and remove likely hiding places for the more nefarious citizens. If urban parks are to be successful, they must be highly accessible and inviting places for us to recreate, which means they must also make us feel safe.

Responses in travel

Tourism is the fastest-growing industry in the world because it can evoke a wonderful sense of adventure and pleasure, which we all seem to crave, but travel can also make us feel very vulnerable.

Following years of bad press due to the perception of high crime, Jamaica decided to address the problem by becoming one of the first to develop the gated resort model. Gated resorts such as Club Med, Sandals and many others have come about in order to address a big part of our travel fears. Gated resorts, like gated communities, are walled compounds, which allow tourists to visit exotic locales—often in developing countries—but avoid any of the potential risks associated with many exotic destinations. Critics of the gated resort idea claim that it dilutes the travel experience and creates even more animosity between tourists and locals.

Cruise ships and cruise holidays are quite similar to gated resorts—a cruise ship is a floating gated resort with a really big moat. Cruise travel, at over $14.5 billion annually, is one of the fastest-growing segments of tourism for a variety of reasons, mostly because it offers a sense of adventure in a highly controlled setting. On a cruise you can see exciting parts of the world from the comfort and security of the ship's deck. If you venture off to shore you are often provided with your own segmented beach seating and guided tours of the local area. No one who is not supposed to be on the ship is on the ship—it is that safe. Though cruise travel appeals to a wide variety of groups it is still most popular with seniors who, coincidentally, also tend to demonstrate the greatest concern with increased crime.

Responses to travel safety fears are most evident where women travelers are concerned. Much as in the workplace, women have played an important part in changing the travel industry. The number of women traveling on their own (especially for business) has dramatically increased since the 1970s. The travel industry recognizes the fact that women are generally more worried about becoming victims of crime, so a variety of innovations have been introduced to alleviate these concerns. For example, many hotels have implemented numberless computerized room keys, the use of passwords for entry into taxis, and, a more recent initiative, uniforming the previously plain-clothed security personnel to provide a more visual sense of security.

The tourism industry knows too well the potential impact that safety concerns may have on its continued business operations. Since the 1950s, safety measures to address personal risk have surfaced in obvious and less obvious design and management initiatives. An example of an obvious measure was taken by the car rental industry in Florida. They began masking rental cars in the early 1990s because it was learned that criminals were targeting marked rental cars leaving airports. Once these travelers left the airport they became easy targets. Rental cars were quickly masked to ensure they could blend in with other cars on the road. Whether it has been through gated resorts, hotel surveillance cameras, masking of rental cars or airport security, measures to address travel fears have changed the tourism industry.

Who Is Most Impacted by Perceptions of Risk?

Not everyone is equally affected by the perception of personal risk. Women in general experience greater fear of victimization, as do elderly and youth populations. Most women and elderly people appear to have accepted a certain amount of lost freedom and choice as a way of life—it has become a leisure constraint as powerful as a lack of time or money. It's seldom discussed because it has become inherent in how we define what it means to be free in the first place.

Youth, on the other hand, appear to have adopted a slightly different approach to perceptions of personal risk: they have become more accepting of violence. Young people, and in the United States young black males in particular, are by far the most victimized. They are growing up in a world where the threat of violence is a fact of everyday life. According to Michael Adams' analysis of attitudes and opinions, today's youth, more than other age groups, have simply come to accept that violence and the threat of violence are a part of everyday life. Time will tell if young people shed this acceptance of violence as they become older and experience life-altering events such as having children or buying a home.

What Is Lost?

Fear of crime and our responses to this fear are likely to be the most important external factors affecting our leisure ability in the future because this fear has redefined what it means to be free. If our fear of crime continues to increase, we could be herded into a very narrow range of safe but limiting lifestyles, always suspicious of what might happen to us and those around us. Stress kills leisure ability and fear of being a victim creates stress as few other threats can.

Chapter References

Adams, Michael. 1998. *Sex in the Snow: Canadian Social Values at the End of the Millennium*. Toronto: Penguin Books.

Fischer, Doug. 1994. "Criminologists say don't panic: Statistics used selectively." Southam News (Ottawa). Reported in the *Calgary Herald* May 15.

Foot, David K., and Stoffman, Daniel. 1996. *Boom Bust and Echo: How to Profit From the Coming Demographic Shift*. Toronto: Macfarlane Walter & Ross.

Krotz, Larry. 1996. *Tourists: How Our Fastest Growing Industry Is Changing the World*. Winchester, MA: Faber and Faber, Inc.

NCPA Policy Report No. 219. August 1998. "Crime and Punishment in America." http://ncpa.org/studies/s219/s219a.html

National Council on the Prevention of Crime. "Picture of Crime in Canada." http://crime-prevention.org/ncpc/council/publications/children/crmfac_e.htm

Pizam, Abraham. 1999. "A Comprehensive Approach to Classifying Acts of Crime and Violence at Tourism Destinations." *Journal of Travel Research*. Vol. 38 (August).

Sonnez, Sevil F.; Yiorgos, Apostolopoulos; and Tarlow, Peter. 1999. "Tourism in Crisis: Managing the Effects of Terrorism." *Journal of Travel Research*. Vol. 38, August, pp.13–18.

Stevenson, Kathryn; Tufts, Jennifer; Hendrick, Dianne; and Kowalski, Melanie. 1999. "Youth and Crime." *Canadian Social Trends*. Statistics Canada, Summer.

Teitel, Jay. 1999. "The Kidnapping of Play." *Saturday Night*, April.

U.S. Department of Justice, Bureau of Justice Statistics. "Victim Characteristics" (Summary Findings). http://www.ojp.usdoj.gov/bjs/cvct_v.htm

• Chapter 8 •

Varying Degrees of Leisure

"**G**et a good education" is a piece of advice that parents have been passing on to children for a long time, and with good reason. We understand that a good education is critical to succeeding in the job market, but education is just as important to our leisure ability. Education can influence many variables in our lives, giving us more freedom of choice and more opportunities for self-expression.

An education allows us to understand, function, integrate, compete and achieve within our present society. It opens doors to our work and career choices and it has the potential to influence our future standard of living, both of which impact our leisure ability. Just how important education is today is reflected in the media, where we see education issues being as vigorously debated as any other political issue. Its importance is reinforced at home—certainly it was in my home. For me, and for many others who grew up in working-class families, education was thought to be the way to level the socio-economic playing field and participate more fully in the society with its wealth of opportunities.

Education and Leisure

Education and leisure come together in several ways. Countless studies on leisure participation have included a specific question asking, "what is the highest level of education you have completed?" We include this when we want to distinguish leisure patterns among different subgroups of the population; that is, age groups, gender, and level of education and income. In each case—and I have seen no contrary results—a clear relationship emerges between how much education one has and her or his level of leisure participation. The more education you have, the more likely you are to participate in leisure activities. People who have completed university tend to have higher participation levels than those with a high school diploma, and those with a high school diploma tend to participate more in leisure activities than those with no diploma. Despite the consistency of these results, seldom is there a reason given for this relationship. Why is leisure participation higher for those with more education?

Having just stated that more education equals more leisure participation, let us stop to consider the completely opposite view offered by Francis Bregha, that education is the force that slowly but steadily erodes our leisure ability and freedom. Francis Bregha claimed that we are only truly free (and able to experience leisure) when we are first born. Once we are old enough to enter pre-school and public school we begin to learn rules that make us conform to the world around us. Slowly we begin to adopt the values and behaviors that narrow our perception of freedom—we begin to integrate into a social structure. We see real examples of this when parents put their child into play school (before public school) so they can learn to play well with other children. It's that structure of rules and expectations that Bregha claims is the first erosion of the pure sense of freedom we had at birth.

In high school, social structure is so important that we conform even more to what is socially accepted. This process of learning and conforming continues through post-secondary schooling and throughout our work lives until retirement when we are once again free, though we may have lost touch by then with what it means to be free.

Are the surveys linking education and increased leisure participation wrong? Is Bregha wrong? No. The surveys measure leisure as participation in a set of recognized leisure activities such as going for walks, reading, gourmet cooking, bird watching and so on. Bregha, on the other hand, wishes to show that pure freedom and our real world of social rules and structure are not always compatible. He makes the point that external factors have a huge impact on our sense of freedom—a point well taken.

Yet most of us understand that we are more or less bound to our social structure and every time we put on our suit and tie or high-heeled shoes, or find ourselves buying into the American Dream, we are reminded of how we accept our social structure. Whether social structure feels constricting or liberating, we live in a society with structure. Education is often the key to finding success within our social structure.

The real power of education is its ability to influence social and economic status and subsequently life's possibilities. It is a powerful tool that also shapes our leisure ability, given that leisure for most of us involves freedom, choice and self-expression *within* our social structure. We can find the influence of education on leisure by looking at how it influences some other important socio-economic factors.

Education and Work

If choice, self-expression and an ability to achieve full capacity are important in our work lives, then education is essential. Young people who don't finish high school experience an unemployment rate that is generally double that of those who have finished high school. Those with a university degree have even lower unemployment rates than those with only a college diploma. People in the high unemployment groups have less opportunity for promotions and lateral mobility and are generally at greater risk of losing their jobs during a period of economic instability. In essence, they have less job security and work-related choice, and experience all the stress-riddled implications that go along with this. Given the way our world works, it appears that more education means more choices and opportunities in our work life. This means a better chance of making more money and finding a job that we really like, which generally results in less stress.

Education and Economic Well-being

Education influences work factors, which have a predictable impact on our economic well-being, all of which affect our leisure ability. Various studies have demonstrated that earning potential increases with more education. We know that people at either end of the economic spectrum experience leisure, but the influence of education is in lessening the potential for money-related stress that comes from being at the low end of the economic spectrum.

Education and Crime

Studies have shown a strong link between low education and the likelihood of involvement in criminal activity. One of the causes of youth crime is reported to be a lack of educational involvement and achievement. Young people who drop out of high school have a greater chance of being involved in criminal activity because a high school dropout is more likely to run straight into high unemployment, unstable and low-paying jobs, and—ultimately—the possibility of living in poverty. Young people living in poverty tend to lose connection with the broader community which, coupled with a sense of invulnerability that comes with being young, adds up to a greater likelihood of eventual criminal involvement.

Education and Opportunities

Despite Bregha's concept that education erodes leisure as pure freedom, it appears that within our society education is the way to open up doors to freedom, choice and self-expression. The value of education to our leisure ability is simple—it's that first door that opens up countless other doors of opportunity in life.

So how much education do you need? The right amount of education depends on your self-image and what you need to do to achieve your full capacity. If it's an astronaut that you want to be, then you need a doctoral degree (maybe two—some of those people are as smart as, well, rocket scientists). If you want to be an accountant, you need less education.

Of course, our self-image can change. Often over the course of one year at college, students will learn that they are in the wrong field and need to change direction. This is often a hard decision because it can appear as though they are waffling, unsure or even stalling—none of which is acceptable in today's productivity-oriented society. Our changing self-image also explains, in part, why so many older adults are now deciding to go back to school. It's our drive to achieve full capacity and avoid stress that ultimately determines how much, if any, education we pursue.

Given that education is so important to our leisure ability we need to take a look at some basic trends and issues affecting education today. Within the myriad of issues surrounding education, our focus will be on three key developments most related to leisure. Depending on your outlook and your personal situation, these trends can be viewed as positive or negative, but each development has an impact.

1. Turning to education

Where there is a choice (excluding public education where enrollments are more about demographics than choice), enrollment in education is increasing. This trend should come as no surprise, given that we are in the midst of an intelligence-based economy. Over the past 20 years enrollments in post-secondary programs have increased in both real and relative terms. The sharpest increase has been in the number of people with a university degree, and in fact, this group has basically tripled in size in that same 20-year period.

Interestingly, it's women who are driving up the numbers, not men. In some cases the enrollment of men in colleges and universities has actually been going down, though overall enrollments are higher because of the high number of women enrolling each year. Also, more university graduates are choosing to get a college diploma to make them even more marketable.

More and more mature students are choosing education. Mature students are those between 25 and 64 years of age who decide to return to school after a significant absence. Mature students are most likely to be in one of two groups: women or men in their late 20s, or women 40 years or older with grown children. Most adults who go back to school do so for work reasons, either related to a present job or future prospects—a point that emphasizes the strong relationship between work and education. Some go back to school simply for personal growth. Regardless of the motivation, more and more mature students are choosing to return to school despite the compromises that must be made when someone does so at an older age. If you or someone close to you have gone back to school as an adult, you know how much of a compromise this involves. At the same time colleges and universities are making the return to school easier by being more flexible in delivering courses and services. For example, distance education and evening, weekend and block-intensive courses are all designed to increase accessibility to schooling.

Education for a mature student is similar to the search for leisure as *freedom from* and *freedom to*—freedom from the stress of finding ourselves under-qualified in a rapidly changing workplace and freedom to obtain the building blocks for more work-related choice, and ultimately achievement of one's full capacity. Whether mature students are looking for more security, wishing to capitalize on workplace changes or have purely personal reasons, the result is usually a positive impact on leisure ability.

2. Controlling education

As long as education has been around there have been parents and others trying to shape it according to what they think is really important. Today, the battle for control of education seems to be more intense, maybe because we realize just how important it is to our future. If education cannot be everything to everyone, then it must at least be what is best, and what is best can be argued to reflect our self-image.

It is important for us to step back and analyze what we are seeking in education and why. We know that education has considerable leverage in shaping our life opportunities, but what does this have to do with leisure? Some people see the present education system as being based on values and goals that are different from theirs, and believe this powerful and influential institution is moving in the wrong direction. What if the values and goals of the education system do not support our own ideal self-image, which we also impose on our children? What choices do we have?

This question is rooted in the reality of everyday discussions that conclude that "a big problem with our society today is our youth," and many would then argue, rightly or wrongly, that the root of the problem is our education system. We hear that schools are too lax or too strict, they are under-funded and can't function or over-funded and need to be trimmed. We hear that teachers have too much power or that teachers are demoralized and not respected. The options, if there is dissatisfaction with the status quo, are threefold, and each option attempts to realign education to more closely match the values, beliefs and self-image of a segment of our society.

The first option is to not interfere in the school system but rather enhance a child's learning at home through more lessons, travel and unique experiences. Many parents probably do this already, out of a basic sense of responsibility. This strategy applies equally to post-secondary students who enhance their learning through summer jobs, volunteering, travel study and non-required elective courses.

The second option involves changing the school system. Here we have several ongoing debates to help present the point: progressive teaching methods versus traditional methods; phonics language learning versus whole language learning; zero tolerance discipline versus alternative discipline strategies; and more parent involvement in decision-making versus more board and government accountability. There are also those who advocate more technology in the classroom, or mandatory second language classes, or greater emphasis on arts versus focusing on the basics, not to mention other contentious debates involving sex education and morning prayers. These debates represent more than a desire to change curriculum or school rules—they represent a movement toward aligning the powerful leverage of education to better reflect our self-image. Even though at some level we know that we cannot custom-design public education to our self-image, we still seek to skew it closer to our own reflection.

For those who are not satisfied with the first two options there's a third. The third option is to take your child out of the standard education system. The decision to opt out of the education system and find an altogether different option has been gaining favor with many families. Opting out of what we would call the basic public school system generally means looking at options like private schools, charter schools and home schooling. Private schools, whether strictly private or private-model, publicly funded charter schools, have become more popular in the past decade, especially schools that have a particular focus such as technology, arts, sports, business, or a religious focus. These schools represent an opportunity to better match the powerful forces of education with a particular set of values. Home schooling has shown dramatic increases in both Canada and the United States in the past 15 years. Home schooling is now legal in all 50 states and countless support organizations are springing up on the Internet. Some families home-school out of necessity, but increasingly home schooling is chosen because parents want their kids to have the type of education that cannot be found in a standard school system, and frequently one that is directly in line with the parents' values and beliefs.

More than elementary, junior and senior high schools, colleges and universities are designed to encourage choice. Programs, majors, minors, electives and even attendance are all subject to choice. Choice is central to the concept of higher education. Yet even at the post-secondary level there are signs of a struggle for control. Universities specifically are a place for learning—traditionally even learning for learning's sake. They have been drawn into a debate that pits the traditional values and merits of a broad education against a market-driven skill focus where employability dominates over knowledge.

3. Increasing responsibility

For a variety of reasons, mainly financial debt, governments reduced or did not increase education funding in the 1990s (this was more the case in Canada than the United States). Local governments, tuition fee increases, business sponsorships and parent fundraising efforts have become important sources of revenue for education all across North America. As governments have given up more and more control of the classroom to parents, corporate partners and others, they have also asked those individuals and communities to play a bigger part in funding education.

While most of us understand that a strong post-secondary education system is needed to build and maintain a vibrant economy and compete globally, we also lean toward the idea that those people who are being educated should shoulder more of the costs of education. Research has shown we believe that a university degree will be critical to succeeding in the workplace of the 21st century, but just over half also believe that the cost of and access to a university degree will become more restrictive during that same time. This trend has two implications for leisure ability.

First, as the cost of education continues to increase it runs the risk of becoming elitist and further widening the gap between the haves and have-nots. The long-term downside of this development to our broader society is both social and economic—social because restricted access to a post-secondary education can create more anxiety and resentment, economic because it will result in a weaker labor pool that ultimately limits economic growth.

Second, the benefits of having more control of the classroom are sometimes offset by the amount of time, money and energy students and parents have to devote to making up for the budget shortfalls. "If you want to dance, you have to pay the fiddler"; if you want more control of the classroom, you have to pay for it.

Throughout North America post-secondary tuition fees skyrocketed in the 1980s and 1990s. At the same time, government reinvestment into post-secondary education has been occurring but it simply hasn't been reflected in the tuition fees. Since the 1995–96 school year state allocations have increased by 28 percent throughout the United States, and 50 percent in California. North of the border, some provinces have reinvested in one-time grants, but overall investment has gone down by 6 percent in that same period. When a college or university education becomes less accessible, so does the positive ripple effect of education on one's lifelong leisure ability.

At the public school level, tuition fees are less of a factor but the effects of government downloading are felt in other ways. Parents are regularly asked to help out at school supervising students, helping teach, cleaning glue bottles and driving students on field trips. Parents now also raise funds for everything from field trips to basic items such as textbooks. For those who want to keep language, art and other programs that are being cut from the curriculum, there are additional costs of money and travel time. In degrees ranging from insignificant to enormous, parents face a growing education-based demand on their time and money.

The Impacts

We know that more and more people are choosing to pursue an education, which is good both for those individuals and for society in general. We also know that as education becomes more important, it is increasingly the object of a control struggle driven by the values and beliefs of different interests. Lastly, an education is becoming harder to get in many cases because of the rising costs involved, and there is no upside to this last trend. Education is at the heart of our society and social structure, and has an important influence on our future social and economic status.

On a personal level, education allows us to better appreciate the world around us, whether that is through the arts, language, the puzzles of science or understanding different cultures. This appreciation can only serve to facilitate our ability to achieve our full capacity. Education also has an important role to play in lessening the gap between the haves and the have-nots. John Kenneth Galbraith in *The Good Society* states that "education has a vital bearing on peace and tranquility; it is education that provides the hope and the reality of escape from the lower, less favored social and economic strata to those above." In our society, if you're educated you have a better chance of living a life that includes freedom, choice and self-expression compared with people who have little or no education. Philosophically and morally, we can argue whether this is right or wrong, but it is inarguably the basic reality of our time.

Chapter References

American Council on Education, 1998. "Straight Talk About College Costs and Prices." *Report of the National Commission of the Cost of Higher Education*, January.

Bernier, Rachel. 1996. "Distance Education: Beyond Correspondence Courses." *Canadian Social Trends*. Statistics Canada, Spring.

Bregha, Francis J. 1991. "Leisure and Freedom Re-examined." In *Recreation and Leisure: Issues in an Era of Change*. State College, PA: Venture Publishing Inc.

Clark, Warren. 1999. "University Graduates at College." *Canadian Social Trends.* Statistics Canada, Autumn.

Galbraith, John Kenneth. 1996. *The Good Society.* New York: Houghton Mifflin Company.

The National Education Goals Panel. 1999. *1999 Key Findings.* http://www.negp.gov./page7-9.htm

Paju, Michael. 1998. "The Class of 90 Goes to Work." *Canadian Social Trends.* Statistics Canada, Summer.

Sanchex, Jorge R., and Laanan, Frankie Santos. 1998. "Assessing the Post-College Earnings of Students: Benefits of Attending California Community Colleges." Paper presented at the Annual Forum of the Association for Institutional Research 38th, Minneapolis MN, May 17–20.

U.S. Census Bureau. 1994. *More Education Means Higher Career Earnings.* SB-94-17.

• Chapter 9 •

The Technology Paradox

A paradox consists of two contradictory statements that appear to collide with one another. The relationship between leisure and technology is built upon a paradox in that technology presents a host of opportunities and a host of threats to leisure, all at the same time. In many cases its rewards are also its costs. A recent Statistics Canada report by Linda Howatson-Leo and Alice Peters on the use of technology neatly captured the paradox that technology presents:

> Those who avail themselves of these technologies have opportunities for expanded access to and participation in the economic, social and cultural life of Canada [and] many Canadians are worried that their skills in using new technologies are inadequate; many people feel they are being out paced by technological developments.

Ever since the early days of human development when the crudest of technological tools were first discovered, we've displayed a child-like fascination with technology. Virtually every innovation throughout history has been met with wide-eyed optimism because we've believed each one could increase our potential as human beings. That is, until recently.

The Technology Train

If technology were a train, it would be a high-speed, high-powered monster of a train, one that's not losing any steam—in fact, it's unstoppable. It's roaring down the track at record speeds and even laying down new track as it goes—it moves like nothing we've seen before. The sheer speed and power of this train are so awesome that they're causing some of its passengers to reach for the emergency stop button. Some of them are scared to ride the train, but they're even more afraid of getting off because they don't want to be left behind.

A candid look at technology would tell us to keep those fears in check because technology has revolutionized our lives for the better. Technology has allowed us to save lives and lessen suffering; it has given us new ways of learning and communicating with one another, opened up outer space and re-engineered our economy. Some of these innovations are more obvious to us now than others; we no longer struggle with finding the merit of less obvious technologies such as the printing press, electricity, the flush toilet and (my favorite) the television remote control. We take these innovations and countless others for granted. The more obvious technologies are usually the ones that have not yet completely settled into our lives—they're still struggling to find a home—and these may include computers, the Internet, genetic technology and the cellphone. New technologies can become old virtually overnight. The fax machine's honeymoon as the new thing has been cut short by newer technologies. It's not a matter of *if* our newest technologies will be taken for granted but *when*.

There is very little today that can match technology in capturing and keeping our interest and awe because it has raised the goal posts of human potential. When we think of leisure as being about self-expression, freedom and achieving our full capacity, the link between the two seems obvious. The first reaction is to connect technology's ability to expand human potential with expanded leisure potential. You don't think that all those track and field records of the 1950s were broken just because we're faster today? It's the shoes! Obviously it's a result of many factors, but what if it was the shoes and what if those shoes were only available to some runners and not others?

The other side of the leisure and technology coin is that while the standard of the possible is being raised, those who do not have the right tools to keep up are left behind. Even those who are connected are not always completely sold on the upside of technology. E-mail and voice-mail make us more efficient but now we get too many of these messages (and some that go on too long). We all struggle with the paradox of technology. There is no doubt that technology has become a dominant force in our lives, but the real question of its impact on our leisure ability is how we relate to technology.

What Technology Means to Leisure

Technology and leisure have a long history together. The earliest tools allowed us to expand our potential and opened new doors to creativity. At the same time those tools made life easier and safer. Agricultural tools allowed us to stay on the land and create food surpluses that eased the harshness of life and fostered the birth of our economy. From the 1600s to the 1800s technology was always defined in association with the arts, crafts and workmanship. Technology had, and continues to have, two basic functions that make it a perfect fit with leisure. The first function is to allow us to achieve more control over the land and the natural world and thus increase our human ability. The second function is to lessen everyday stress and make life more safe and livable. The two functions are similar to leisure as *freedom to* and *freedom from*.

Leisure can be viewed as freedom to become the person we have the ability to become and freedom from the stress and oppression of daily life. We can review virtually any list of technological innovations and categorize them as econtributing to either *freedom to* or *freedom from*.

Virtual reality technology, whereby a completely realistic but artificial environment is created, expands our *freedom to* side through games, training and virtual travel. That same technology may be used (in the future), on the *freedom from* side, to do remote medical diagnostic assessments. Imagine an injured mountain climber halfway up Mount Everest putting on a virtual reality suit and being examined by a doctor in Los Angeles. A more everyday example is the titanium golf club we use to add distance to our drive (freedom to achieve more) and the lightweight Gore-Tex suit we use to stay dry and warm while we golf in the rain (freedom from).

The upside to technology is clear. The downside occurs when the pace of change that technology brings is so great that it interferes with our lives rather than enhancing them. Or when technology brings about an ability that we don't really know how to deal with, such as genetic technology and life-support technologies. Technology is a tool—no more, or less—and it can have a positive impact on our leisure ability or it can create anxieties and stress, which kill our leisure ability.

Let's go back to the technology-train analogy. It's clear that this train has done a tremendous amount of good along its journey. Once it passes a town, that town is changed forever, and usually for the better. The scary part about this train is as it gains more and more speed and lays down new tracks, we begin to wonder who is actually driving this train—is it a small (virtual) community of engineers who can't relate to most of us out here? I don't think there is a single answer to this question because each one of us answers it every day as we navigate through technology and experience good and bad days. On the good days, technology provides the security and innovation that enhances our leisure ability. On bad days we feel frightened, overwhelmed or annoyed by it, resulting in a stress that hinders our leisure ability. Each one of us has a different view of technology and how it impacts our lives.

In order for us to focus on the innovations that now impact us most, we need to define some parameters for our discussion of technology. First is a simple acknowledgment that we all use technology in some way (as you're reading this book you're using several different technologies). The second is that most of the technology in our lives we now take for granted. These basic technologies are too numerous to mention and will be treated as a given in our discussion. The third is that our discussion will focus on the newer technologies.

Who's Wired and Who's Not

With respect to the newer technologies, you can probably guess what type of person is most likely to be a happy passenger (if not a driver) on the technology train. This person would be younger and most likely in the 15 to 24 age group, or perhaps in the 25 to 45 age group. This person is well educated and financially well off and probably living in a household that earns more than $50,000 a year ($75,000 in Canada). In this household we are likely to find a spouse and children, although the person who spends more than six hours a week on the Internet is usually single. This person is more likely to use computers and related technology at work and is also more likely to be urban. Not surprisingly, most of us share at least some of these characteristics, which reflects the widespread use of new technologies.

We cannot answer the question of who's wired and who's not without making a distinction in the type of technology we are talking about. We're not talking about Mac versus PC. We are talking about everyday household technologies versus computer and Internet technologies. The difference between the two is based on choice and consequences. We generally have more choice and fewer downside consequences in our decisions about everyday household technologies. We have less and less choice (and more downside consequences) when it comes to our decisions about whether to get connected to the Internet or not. That important element of choice can have a big impact on our leisure ability.

Everyday Household Technology

Household timesaving technology is most used by time-stressed dual-earner families where both adults work. Within this group, the overwhelming majority use such items as the microwave oven, dishwasher, VCR, compact disc player, and about 7 out of 10 even own two or more television sets. Dual-earner households are also much more likely to be affluent and more likely to have children living at home—all factors that add to the likelihood of embracing technology. George Jetson and his space-age family we are not, but we're not homesteaders either. We have grown to be very comfortable with the myriad of timesaving devices we have at our disposal—to the point where most of us take them for granted. It took an event such as the Y2K scare for us to realize how much we have come to rely on everyday household technology and how deeply uncomfortable (and even frightening) was the prospect of living without it.

We must assume that household technology enhances everyday life because despite advertising pressure, we can choose to use these technologies or not with little real consequence. Many of us have chosen to go without certain household technologies such as automatic dishwashers, television sets and even answering machines. While most of us have choice when it comes to household technology, choice is less of a reality when it comes to some other forms of technology.

Computers and the Internet

Tracking the use and spread of technology today essentially means tracking the use of computers and the Internet. According to Michael Dertouzos, author of *What Will Be: How the New World of Information Will Change Our Lives*, the most profound impacts of technology on our society will come from computers, software and the supporting infrastructure (that is, the tools and services that enable activities to go on). It's no wonder that our fascination with technology seems to revolve around the world of computers.

Today just under half of all North Americans are connected on the Internet either at home, at work or at school. Many of us are connected in more than one place. The technology behind computers has improved by leaps and bounds as well. Today, a typical notebook computer has as much computing power as a mainframe computer did in the early 1980s. At the same time we're witnessing corporate mergers bringing together the companies that provide fiber optics, cable services and the content—such as the news, entertainment and e-commerce—behind those services. The industry is building itself to further expand in depth and breadth. The imperative around computer and Internet use is felt in many areas, but two more than others—small business and e-commerce.

Throughout the 1990s in North America the engine behind our economy has been the small business sector. This sector relies on and arguably has been propelled by new developments in computer and Internet technology. It has been their leverage when going up against the giants, and the message is pretty clear—if you're a small business you had better be completely wired or you're not going anywhere. Regardless of what you're selling, being an entrepreneur today means that you are either highly computer literate or (like me) you have a great computer support person nearby.

E-commerce, or electronic commerce, refers to financial and business-to-business transactions that are carried out over the Internet, and it seems poised to have the biggest impact on how we work and live. E-commerce was estimated at $1.3 billion in Canada in 1999 and over $38 billion in the United States and it is likely to grow to $350 billion by 2002 in the United States. E-commerce is also changing the way we shop (according to one advertisement we can now "shop naked") and it is forcing all types of businesses to re-engineer themselves to open up virtual storefronts in anticipation of real shoppers.

When it comes to leisure ability, the one problem with e-commerce is that it is not nearly so universally used as many thought it would be by now. The typical e-commerce shopper is a younger, well educated and financially well off person who is also most likely to be single. It's a person with above average means, which implies that the majority of the population, especially those who are less educated and well off, are excluded.

Technology has brought about innumerable changes to daily life. In some cases we've had more choice than in others. In some cases these choices have been a blessing and in others a blight, but there's no doubt that technology impacts the way we live and our ability to experience leisure. As I researched various impacts, the technology paradox was repeatedly reinforced by examples of technology enhancing, and complicating, our lives. The paradox is unavoidable, which means that we have to look at each example from both a personal and collective point of view to see both sides of the situation.

Technology and Globalization

Those who have gained control of technology and the global economy have managed to harness two monstrous powers that have reshaped much of our world. Globalization has the most relevant impact as it relates to our leisure. The global economy means that the world is one big shopping mall with no borders. Globalization has been the basis for most of the economic growth of the past decade, as it creates countless new opportunities and expands old ones for companies and individuals.

The other side of globalization is less rosy. A global economy means that business works around the clock and that means we too are beginning to work around the clock, whether we want to or not.

Working Around the Clock

Technology has changed the way we work in countless ways, but most important to leisure is our ability to work any time and anywhere. Depending on your own personal situation, the changes brought about by computers and communication technology are either liberating or suffocating, or both.

Basic technology support for the telephone and videoconferencing has allowed us to be more efficient. Critical decisions requiring a number of people in real time can be set up in an instant. A CEO can now videoconference an important message to hundreds of offices around the globe, also in real time. The Internet, e-mail, fax machines, and even cellphones and pagers give us the freedom to set up home-based businesses, to telecommute and to create virtual offices.

Personal computers, teleconferencing and telecommuting can give us more leisure ability because of the freedom and flexibility they offer. At the same time these tools have increased the speed of work, whether that means the time it takes to get a report done, the research behind the report or making and communicating decisions. Not only do we work faster, we now have the ability to work more, because we can work anywhere and any time. (If someone e-mails a question to me at eleven o'clock at night, am I expected to answer it then?)

The workplace sometimes sends mixed messages. On the one hand balance in the new millennium is all-important—not just for the employee but for the success of the company. On the other hand, it falls over itself in giving us new ways to stay connected through e-mail access at home, cellphones and beepers, computer notebooks, palmtops and more. This makes it harder to leave work behind and sends the message that if you're at all important to the company, you need to be ready to work anywhere and any time. Technology allows work to encroach more and more on our lives in an informal way. Some of the "work encroachment" is driven by the simple competitiveness of the global economy which does not recognize time zones (such as the proposed global stock market amalgamation that will result in a 24-hour-a-day, 7-day-a-week stock market). Some is driven by job insecurity—we feel we have to constantly demonstrate our value. When technology makes us feel more stressed by pressuring us to work more and not leave our work behind it takes away from our leisure ability.

Technically Safe

Today we use simple technology in all sorts of ways to make us and those around us feel safe. We will lend our cellphones to our kids and older parents if we think they might risk any sort of trouble. Video surveillance cameras at our schools, workplaces and hotels make us feel safer and they have been successful in catching many of the culprits who otherwise would have escaped. Home security systems have a similar effect as a proactive technology-based safety measure. Global positioning systems (GPS) keep us from getting lost in the jungle—even the concrete jungle, if one has been installed in our new car.

Technology allows us to feel connected—whether it is through our laptop computer, beeper, cellphone, parking lot video camera or home security system—and that makes us feel safer. The upside is the safer we feel the more likely we are to act on our desires and the more likely we are to experience leisure. The downside is that maybe we will rely on technology for security in place of our own judgment. This is easy to do. Park rangers are increasingly worried about the growing numbers of people who travel into the backcountry poorly prepared but carrying a cellphone—and then rely on it in place of their own judgment and expertise should they encounter any trouble. However, technology allows us to feel connected with others, which allows us to feel safer, and that means less stress. Less stress means more leisure ability.

Education

The influence of technology on education has been enormous, but it's still unclear whether the impact has been good or bad. Advocates of technology will tell you that distance learning, computer-assisted learning, Internet research capabilities and computer-simulated learning have all made education easier and more accessible. There is no doubt that with the help of technology many people receive an education they otherwise would not receive. Today you can buy software to teach you just about anything. On the other hand, some claim that the enormous emphasis placed on technology in our schools has shifted resources and focus away from the basic learning process.

If we go back to our Chapter 8 discussion on education, we will recall that the one thing that makes education so important to our leisure is that it allows for maneuvering throughout our social structure. Whether we think it's right or not, those who are educated have more opportunities in this world and those who are computer experts (or even computer literate) have more opportunities than those who are not.

The Way We Play

Show me ten serious hard-core outdoor enthusiasts and I'll show you at least nine who are tech-junkies. Few types of play have been so influenced by technology as has outdoor adventure recreation. Technology has allowed virtually anyone to conquer the outdoors. We don't venture into the wilderness today without being covered in extraordinarily well functioning synthetic rain and wind gear, ergonomically designed backpacks, lightweight tents and cooking stoves that resemble chemistry lab equipment (not to mention the backcountry espresso-maker). Technology has meant that virtually anyone among us can access the wilderness in ways we never dreamed possible just a few short decades ago.

Put yourself back in the 1940s when downhill skiing was being introduced to North America, when skis were no more than two wooden planks you could tie to your boots and skiing down hill meant you had to *walk up* hill first. Today technology has given us the simple chairlift, only to be updated by the high-speed quadruple detachable chairlift, so we get zoomed up the mountain at great speeds in order to minimize the amount of time we spend on the chair. Still, while on the chair we stay warm in our Gore-Tex clothing and battery-warmed ski boots. We managed to upgrade our skis from wooden planks to fiberglass, metal-edged skis to the shaped (hour-glass) ski to help the aging baby boomers continue to make their turns, to the Smart Ski with its own computer guidance system. Technology is redefining what we can do.

Most of us see the benefits of technology's ability to make the outdoors more accessible. But many people argue that we don't need to make the outdoors more accessible, that we already have too many people on the ski hills, rivers, lakes and trails. That something as simple as the commercial inflatable river raft has opened up pristine rivers to hordes of trampling, noisy visitors—and that too is the impact of technology. We have gained a greater sense of confidence in our mastery over the natural world. It's allowed us to go farther, faster and to places we never could have before—and some would argue it's given us a false sense of confidence.

Clearing up the Paradox

There are as many examples of technology supporting our leisure ability as there are of its hindering leisure. How do we assess technology's impact on our leisure ability in a way that makes its impact clear? The key is to under-stand how you fit into the broader trends, and only two really matter.

The first major trend is all about empowerment. It's about the power to expand potential and the ways in which technology is redistributing the power that's there. The second trend is that while all these exciting changes are going on there is still only a small of group people who are really in the driver's seat. The rest of us either hang on for dear life or we're left behind completely.

Paul Hoffert refers to the empowering aspect of technology as the "bagel effect"—that is, technology decentralizes the traditional power base to virtually anyone (shifting power from the inside of the bagel circle to the outside of the circle). The decentralizing effect is most evident in business where the Internet presents clear competitive advantages. The bagel effect allows small companies to compete with large multinationals. It also allows consumers access to a greater range of products and services, thereby giving them more overall power and clout in the marketplace. Internet technology, specifically, has given individuals power that was previously the exclusive domain of large corporations and institutions.

If leisure is about freedom, self-expression and achieving full capacity (and it is) then this trend of decentralizing power certainly enhances our leisure ability. Everyone from the new wave of dot-com millionaires, to the grandmother living in Anchorage who's finishing her graduate degree at Stanford via Internet, to the community activist fighting to get support for a new playground has realized some of what this potential has to offer. So where's the downside?

For every one of us who's completely wired and ready to change the world, there are likely two others who might be wired but are struggling and stressing over the challenges of getting on board and another two who believe they have no chance of ever getting on board. Technology is simply not as accessible as some people would like to believe. But most of us are neither on the leading edge nor completely left behind—we are in the middle group that regularly struggles to stay on board. The net effect of technology for us must be presumed to be positive inasmuch as it allows us to better address everyday worries and propels us to find new and better ways to achieve our full capacity.

Chapter References

Dertouzos, Michael. 1997. *What Will Be: How the New World of Information Will Change Our Lives.* New York: HarperEdge / HarperCollins Publishers Inc.

Duffy, Andrew. 2000. "Web serves affluent best: Access out of reach for many low income earners." Report on POLLARA poll in the *Calgary Herald*. January 16.

Hoffert Paul. 1998. *The Bagel Effect.* Toronto: McGraw-Hill Ryerson.

Howatson-Leo, Linda, and Peters, Alice. 1997. "Everyday Technology: Are Canadians Using It?" *Canadian Social Trends*. Statistics Canada, Autumn.

McInerney, Francis, and White, Sean. 2000. *Futurewealth: Investing in the Second Great Wave of Technology*. New York: St Martin's Press.

Productivity Policy Institute. "E-commerce Takes Off."
http://www.neweconomyindex.org/section3_page04.html

Productivity Policy Institute. "More Businesses on the Net."
http://www.neweconomyindex.org/section3_page04.html

Productivity Policy Institute. "More Schools on the Internet."
http://www.neweconomyindex.org/section3_page06.html

Samuel, Nicole. 1996. "Technology Invades Leisure." *World Leisure and Tourism*. World Leisure and Recreation Association. Vol. 38, No. 3.

Chapter 10

Governing Our Leisure

The institution of government has been with us throughout the ages but few of us are aware of its impact on our leisure ability. To understand this impact we need to go back to the two basic parts of leisure: *freedom to* become the person we have the ability to become—to achieve our full capacity—and *freedom from* the stress and oppression of daily life.

We're not likely to rely on government to make our dreams come true and to have our full capacity achieved because these are things that we have to do ourselves. However, we may rely on government to provide us with some opportunities for leisure, like the local city-run pool or the national park we visit from time to time.

If its role on the *freedom to* side is limited, then what about the *freedom from* side—freedom from everyday stress and oppression? Police, fire, ambulance, transportation, safety, medical, military, social services—these are just some of the functions of government most of us rely on. These functions prevent serious danger, make us feel safer, and help us in those instances when we need help the most. They work to free us from the stress and oppression of everyday life to allow us to experience leisure.

Is There a Department of Leisure?

The answer is no, not really. Government in general is in the business of quality of life. Everything it does is supposed to improve our quality of life, which enriches leisure. Certain parts of government play a more direct role in our search for leisure. For instance, most parks, whether national or local, are run by government. Local government plays an important role in providing an array of programs and services (recreation, education, arts, social support and so on) that may facilitate our leisure. Government is also involved in tourism through the promotion of destinations, transportation regulation or provision of travel advisories. Government provides a great range of leisure-supporting services, and most are focused on the *freedom from* aspect of leisure. For instance, when you're traveling abroad on vacation the only place you're likely to run into your government is at the Embassy if you need help or at the border when arriving home.

Today, we accept that government has a part to play in leisure, and more specifically in recreation and tourism. Most of us accept this largely because this is the way it's been for generations.

Government and Leisure

It would be hard for us to pinpoint exactly when government got involved in leisure. We would have to go back to the days of the ancient Greeks and Romans, when the authorities of the day built public baths, public gardens and stadiums. Even then initiatives were somewhat controversial; most were torn down during the Dark Ages that followed.

Looking at more recent history, we could go back to the Industrial Age in Europe during the 1800s to find an important development—parks. As a way to make life more bearable, governments developed urban parks so people could escape the gray city life and reconnect with nature. National parks in the United States and Canada began in the west, in the late 1880s. Their mandate of preservation and enjoyment is much the same today as it was then.

If few of us live near a national park, there are other types of services we use more often. Inner-city parks, pools, ball diamonds, soccer fields, ice rinks and so on are the types of government services that are likely to have a more direct impact on our day-to-day leisure. The underlying goal of government-provided facilities has always been to provide basic opportunities that will make life a little easier.

Since the 1990s—and in some states even earlier—most government leisure services have been going through a huge transformation from what we call "apple pie and motherhood" status to a business status. Government leisure services from the 1960s to the 1980s were seen as something so precious and sacred that they were never questioned. Seldom did they come under the budget-cutting knife because their value was recognized to be high.

Today most government leisure providers have had to contend with an onslaught of competition from the not-for-profit and commercial sectors while addressing budget cuts to their own programs and services. This has led to a shift in government leisure.

Shifting Government Leisure

Since the early 1990s, it can be argued that government-sponsored leisure has shifted away from its traditional focus on supporting *freedom from* to a focus on competing in the marketplace. When these types of services have to compete in the marketplace they are less likely to subsidize users of the services because they need to make a profit. This means they become more difficult for some people to access because of cost.

The best way to see this shift is though a basic model called the "leisure services continuum." It's a simple model that has been around for many years and it is still widely used. The model states that there are essentially three levels of leisure services or goods that we get from the government: public, merit and private levels of service. These levels are determined by two basic criteria: who benefits from the type of service provided, and who has to pay for the service provided. Using this simple model we can track just how government leisure services have shifted away from their original purpose of supplying opportunities for everyone.

Criteria	Public Level	Merit Level	Private Level
Who benefits from this service?	Everyone benefits	Everyone, but the user more	Just the user benefits
Who pays for this service?	Everyone pays	Everyone, but the user more	Just the user pays

Let me give you an example to illustrate how this model works. Consider the National Park system, which is a government-sponsored leisure opportunity. They provide all three levels of service: public, merit and private.

At the public level we all benefit and we all pay, not through fees but through our taxes. For the National Park system the public level of service is the benefit we get from knowing that there are parks and other important places set aside for conservation and enjoyment—the service is the knowledge. We benefit from this knowledge in a peace-of-mind kind of way and we pay for this peace of mind through our taxes. Everyone benefits in that we *can* visit the park if we want to. The fact that we can visit our national parks means that it's another opportunity available to us, even if we go only once in our lives—it's still an option.

Let me give you an example of how this type of thinking sometimes works. When I conducted a quality of life study for my home town of Calgary, I found that "living next to the mountains" was one of the most popular responses to the question of what adds to one's quality of life. This was interesting because most of these people only go to the mountains a couple of times a year (they are about an hour away). The benefit is not that they go frequently, but that they are able to go to the mountains when they choose to.

The merit-level service the national parks provide is based on the idea of user-pay. When we actually visit one of our national parks in Canada or the United States and we *use* the park first-hand, we usually have to pay a gate fee (in addition to our taxes). The idea is that if we're using the park, we benefit more than other people who don't, so we have to pay more than just our taxes. Even though the gate fee does not pay for the whole cost of our visit, it helps to offset the cost.

Now, once we're in the park and we've paid our gate fee, we may want to take advantage of some of their more specialized government-run services, like swishing around in a hot pool. This type of service is usually run at the private level: *only* the user is seen to benefit so only the user pays. It's pretty hard to convince the rest of the country that they're benefiting from you swishing around a hot pool.

This model also holds true for a whole range of local government leisure services. The public parks in your city are examples of the public level of service because everyone benefits and everyone pays. The local swimming pool may be a merit-level service if you have to pay a small admission fee to get in, and the local golf course—if it's run by the city—is probably an example of a private-level service because golf fees pay for the full cost of its operation.

The Shift

What we've witnessed since the early 1990s is that government services have moved to the right of the continuum. They have generally shifted from the public level to the merit level and from the merit level to the private level. With each shift, the cost of the service to the consumer goes up rather than to the taxpayer at large. Think of a pool that you used to swim at for free, but that now you have to pay to use. Imagine the fees at that same pool rising even higher now because the City can't afford to subsidize it any longer. As government leisure providers have experienced the impacts of rising competition and falling budgets, they have started to require their facilities to bring in revenue wherever possible. This has generally meant shifting to the right of the continuum.

The shift to the right could mean many things to each one of us. For some people it's a good news story because they fully believe in the user-pay idea and they don't want to pay for anything they don't use. A move to the right of the continuum usually means that fewer of our tax dollars go to support these types of services. The shift may also mean that poor people with little or no disposable income have fewer opportunities to recreate and rejuvenate. A fee increase, even a small one, may be more of a mental barrier than a real financial barrier, but it may still be enough to prevent a young family from visiting the local rink or pool. What the shift really means to those who are poor, even the working poor, is more stress, not less. This adds to the stress of everyday life and therefore makes leisure that much less likely. In this way it takes away from our leisure ability.

Does It Matter?

When all is said and done, government-sponsored leisure services clearly occupy a unique position in relation to our leisure ability. They give us opportunities to find *freedom from* our daily stress and oppression. Even though these basic services may not be as sexy or exciting as many others, they are still very important because they guarantee a base level of leisure ability. Maybe the fact that they are public (meaning we all own them) is the reason we feel that the local park is an extension of *our* backyard and the local pool *our* family pool.

Alleviation of some of life's daily stresses is how we expect government to assist us in our search for leisure. When government is less able to carry out this function we are more likely to encounter stresses that impede leisure ability.

Chapter References

Brimacomb, Doug, and Fink, H. 1981. "Public and Private Leisure Services: A Case Study." *Recreation Canada*, December.

Hamilton Ross Systematics. 1996. *1996 Alberta Recreation Survey.*

Searle, Mark S., and Brayley, Russell E. 1993. *Leisure Services in Canada*. State College, PA: Venture Publishing Inc.

Rediscovering Leisure

Chapter 11

Moving Toward Seamless Living

If we have learned anything about leisure in the past 20 years, it's that our notion of leisure has changed and that external factors can have an impact on the type and amount of leisure we experience. However, that has not dampened our curiosity about the basic question, *Do we have more or less leisure now than in the past?*

We are curious about how much leisure we have for a variety of reasons. The amount and degree of leisure we have is a measure of quality of life, and it is also a way to mark changes over time. We also want to know how much leisure we have because while most of us have heard about the predictions of more leisure time, we just don't believe it—it doesn't *feel* as if we have any more leisure. These are all good reasons to revisit the question, and it's time to do so with the tools we now have at our disposal.

Our first new tool is an updated definition of leisure as "the experience of living in a moment of positive self-expression." This definition will make it more difficult to answer our question because it is not easy to measure, but anything less will simply not do. The other tool is our understanding of the impacts various trends can have on our leisure ability. With these tools in hand, we are adequately armed to tackle this question.

Timing the Human Race

The phrase conjures up images of a stopwatch-wielding coach with a line of runners at the ready, or the rush-hour commutes where many of us are racing to find the fastest path from point A to point B. But this implies that time is involved.

Time is commonly defined as the measurement of an object through space. You can visualize a brick falling from a tall building and think of its travel to the ground as the measure of time. The measurement of an object through space implies a direct and focused point-A-to-point-B type of path with no stops.

Perhaps we are the objects and we are traveling through the space of our lives. It's an image that lends itself to a description of the pace of life some days—a brick falling from a tall building; a lifestyle that is on a direct and focused path with few stops along the way. All too often life feels harried and lacking in the richness that a few of those stops could offer. However, leisure as self-expression and the achievement of full capacity does not fit the timing of the human race image. In fact, it implies a meandering route instead of a direct route; rather than a focus on the timing of the race, it implies a focus on the satisfaction gained within the racecourse.

How Much Free Time Do We Have?

For those people who still wish to cling to the notion of leisure time, the prognosis is not very good. Research on whether we have more or less leisure time now than in the past is not conclusive. That is, some claim we have a little more free time now while others claim we have less now than we did in the past. Most agree that whether you have more or less leisure time has a lot to do with your age and the specific circumstances in your life.

Furthermore, most agree that those of us between 25 and 45 (maybe as high as 55), with children, who are working full time or close to full time, have *less* free time now than in the past. This group is most susceptible to the stresses of modern living. One of these stresses is the need to adopt a variety of different roles (parent, career person, volunteer, caregiver to older parents and so on). Each role we take on adds a little more to our time stress. As well, members of the younger end of this group are likely to be the big spenders (not out of choice but out of necessity) on items such as a first house, new car, student loans, furniture, baby items and so on. This group is well acquainted with financial stress and they have little, if any, free time. Parents of young children are on duty around the clock and the stresses of the intense demands of this period in life may also make any free time that *is* available stress-filled.

The 15 to 24 age group has seldom been studied in terms of the amount of leisure time they have. Since the early 1950s, they have been assumed to be students leading an idyllic life. Given the cost of education, more and more students are now working and going to school at the same time, so we have to assume that the amount and quality of their leisure time has been compromised. If they're not out there finding tuition money, many are working to buy the newest clothes and accessories (which now of course includes a cellphone) just to keep up with the crowd. Youth have never been the target of big business interests to the extent they are today.

In addition to time constraints, youth are also increasingly pressured to succeed in a career and financial sense. I see this pressure in many of the students I teach at university. They are driven to get the grade that gets them into the right program that gets them into the right job that makes them "successful." On its own, this pressure is not necessarily good or bad, but it is a sign that many of them are eager to follow the baby boomers on the harried path that many boomers are now seriously reconsidering. Youth today show more signs of being both time-stressed and just plain stressed.

Which group might have more free time now than in the past? The obvious answer is seniors, or those who are generally 65 years and older. At present seniors make up a fairly small proportion of our society, but beginning in 2011, when the first baby boomers turn 65, this group will represent about one in three North Americans. On average, today's seniors have more money and education than previous seniors, and both are factors that contribute to more leisure time. Seniors of today who were born prior to the 1940s are likely to experience more leisure time than their predecessors. A robust economy and medical and travel technology advances, among other factors, indicate that this group may have more leisure time. The question is whether they know how to enjoy their time; this is a group that has grown up with a strict work ethic and a tendency to associate leisure with idleness.

Perhaps the most likely group to find and enjoy leisure time is our current crop of baby boomers as they turn into seniors. The optimists among us would claim that these seniors will experience a lot of free time. Others might argue that real and meaningful leisure doesn't just suddenly happen when we turn 65 and stop going to work every morning. As Francis Bregha pointed out, many of us have become so entrenched in the structure of our lives that by the time we reach retirement age, we have forgotten what freedom and self-expression feels like. Not everyone who retires does so with a smile on their face; some people are afraid to leave work because they don't know what to do with themselves after work. But today's baby boomers are showing signs of great wisdom. Increasingly, those who can afford to are choosing to downscale and live simpler lifestyles. Their lives tend to take on more diverse interests that can be maintained long after people stop working for a living.

In the broad survey of who has more or less leisure time, the unemployed and poor are a group with obvious free time but equally obvious stresses, which negate the enjoyment of their free time. This group is likely to have as much free time now as their predecessors, but their stress levels may be higher today with the widening of the gap between the rich and poor. It has always been hard to be poor, but it may be harder to be poor and unemployed when the daily news is filled with stories of skyrocketing financial markets and record corporate profits. Stress takes the "free" out of free time.

As we have seen, we cannot measure leisure time or free time without considering the personal meaning of that time. Even if we could calculate the amount of free time we have now compared with previous generations, it is only a mathematical calculation of time and may not have anything to do with true leisure. The question of whether we have more or less leisure now than in the past must be addressed within the context of the meaningful definition of leisure that we now have. It is through this definition that we will be able to personally answer our question of whether we have more or less leisure.

What Does More Leisure Even Look Like?

If we're supposed to have more leisure, but it doesn't feel as if we do, then maybe we are not using the right criteria to measure. We need to drop the notion that time is the definitive measure of our leisure and settle on new measures or criteria that actually measure leisure as it is really experienced. This will not be easy because we've been conditioned to think of leisure as time, and because the real and meaningful measures are more abstract and personal than a calculation of free time. Nonetheless, we have to continue to rethink leisure and what it means to us individually. One of the ways we can do this is to try to imagine what more leisure (as we have defined it) might actually look like in our present-day world.

What would more leisure look and feel like? We would know that we had more leisure **if our lives were characterized by acts of self-expression that brought us closer to being the person we want to be; if we felt a greater ability to live in the moment, being present and connected in everyday life, with less stress.**

Guided by **a strong and clear self-image**, our first criterion, we experience an array of opportunities to achieve our full capacity—to be the type of parent, friend, partner, employee, volunteer and so on that we ideally want to be. What it means to achieve full capacity is deeply personal. If it is based on an image we are pressured into by the people around us, or the powerful media messages we see every day we'll find ourselves chasing someone else's image and not our own. For instance, people who pursue financial success with no clear personal goals that ground the success can find themselves feeling empty. Once our leisure goals are in place, we can turn our attention to negotiating external factors to achieve those goals, or at least move in the right direction.

Freedom to become the person we have the ability to become is an important criterion in assessing our leisure position, but we cannot neglect the subtle aspects of the journey that brings us there. A common approach is to forgo the present for the future—our journey becomes filled with self-denial and sacrifice for a later prize. Therefore our second criterion is that **we are** actually living in the moment, that we are present and connected with the people, environment and events around us as we strive to achieve our full capacity.

Of the two measures of leisure we've looked at so far—ability to achieve our full capacity and ability to live in the moment—the latter appears to be much harder to achieve. We can find a lot of type A, driven personalities (and we have many of those) who have a good idea of what to do to achieve their full capacity, but living in the moment seldom makes it on the day's to-do list. The challenge is to find a balance between the two.

"Do we have a greater ability to live in the moment today than others did 20 years ago?" is a question more reflective of true leisure. Pause to consider your ability to live in the moment you are in. The harried and pressure-filled circumstances of life today make living in the moment hard to do, yet it is still an undeniable measurement of our leisure. Therefore we need to add to our list of criteria **freedom from the greatest barrier to living in the moment—stress.** Stress is the discomfort that results when our expectations do not match reality. We seek freedom from stress because it can derail our best intentions and taint just about anything we are doing or feeling. Stress can also create such preoccupation that we delay doing the things we value, such as going back to school in later life, changing jobs or taking an important trip.

Whether you have more or less leisure now and in the future is based on three criteria:

- your opportunities to achieve your full capacity
- your ability to live in the moment
- how stress-free your experience is

How would you rate your leisure based on these three measures?

The Roles of Stress

One of the more noticeable developments of the last 30 years in North America has been our ability and desire to take on different roles. For instance, a woman of the 1950s was pretty much limited to the roles of a wife, mother, homemaker and maybe a part-time worker. Some women broke the molds to become community and corporate leaders, but they were the exception and not the rule. Men similarly led fairly focused lives anchored by their role as the breadwinner, followed by husband and father. Life's energies were focused on fewer roles, thereby increasing the sense of control over life and free time.

Times have changed and today a woman can be a wife, mother and homemaker, as well as a corporate and community participant or leader. Men have kept the breadwinner role but they have a bigger part to play as husband, father and community member. Playing more and distinctly different roles means that life gets complicated and stressful because all these different roles are hard to balance—especially if we expect to be really good at them, too.

Having multiple roles presents a double-edged sword for our leisure ability and for the way we run our race through life as we get pulled in different directions. Our racecourse is no longer a straight line, but a meandering one that takes more energy to run but is probably more enjoyable and satisfying for many of us. It's harder to live life as a mother, wife, career person, community leader and caregiver to older parents than it is to be just one or two of those, but whether we do so by choice or not, more and more of us have taken on these multiple roles. This means more of us are on this meandering racecourse but, despite the richness multiple roles can bring, we are no longer satisfied with being pulled in so many different directions.

This brings us to two important developments gleaned from the trends we have discussed in the previous section. The first is the opportunity to live more seamless lives, where our multiple roles become intertwined with one another and with our self-image. The second is the challenge we face since certain trends make seamless living hard to achieve for many of us.

Seamless Living

The trend toward seamless living appears to be growing out of an *angst* that arguably started with dissatisfaction from having too narrow a range of roles back in the 1950s and '60s. This angst was addressed by expanding the range of roles men and women could take on in the 1970s. By the 1980s we were fully immersed in lifestyles based on multiple roles and by the 1990s, angst once again began to grow as we realized that living this way was just about killing us. We are not prepared to give up our roles but we are also desperately seeking ways to ease the stress of being pulled in so many different directions.

Enter seamless living. Seamless living is not about reaching a superficial type of success portrayed in glossy magazine advertisements. It's about being able to take on as many roles as we want and still feel that we are accomplishing something in each role, and that the combined efforts of all roles are bringing us closer to achieving our full capacity. Seamless living is the backlash to feeling as if we're traveling through life harried and disconnected.

The desire to seamlessly weave together the activities of all our roles is a big shift in terms of how we want to live, and today's trends are pointing us in that direction. Work is becoming more integrated with the rest of our lives. For instance, alternative work arrangements such as flex-time and telecommuting are designed to minimize the seam between the work and non-work parts of our lives. Education leaves, workplace child care, and workplace fitness and recreation centers also help to eliminate the work and non-work seam.

Technology has played a critical role in facilitating seamless living. Many of us can work from home as easily as we can from the office, thereby diminishing the seam. We now feel the latitude to leave the office to deal with family emergencies or medical appointments because we remain connected and productive. Technology has also been instrumental in allowing those people who want to live in rural parts of the country (an important act of self-expression for some people) to do so and stay connected.

The personal computer is a good example of how we have started to seamlessly weave together the different roles we carry out. From one terminal in the course of one evening we can do some leftover work from the office, research a topic for our night class, buy a birthday gift for Mom and have it shipped to her house, and chat with friends through e-mail. Activity related to all sorts of different roles can be carried out with one tool in a virtually seamless manner.

Every generation witnesses one or two major trends that sweep through society and change the way we live—for instance, the baby boom and consumerism of the 1940s and 1950s, redrafted social values of the 1960s and 1970s, the green revolution of the 1980s. I would argue that we are now at the cusp of seamless living. The idea of seamless living bodes well for our leisure ability and it might be a sign of true leisure in the future. There are few ways that the concept of leisure as living in a moment of positive self-expression can be realized better than through seamless living. The challenge is overcoming the host of trends that make seamlessness more difficult to attain.

The downside of many of the trends we examined in Section Two is the increasing amounts of stress many of us experience in one or more of our roles. Consider the effects of globalization on our personal sense of control over our livelihood, less disposable income for low-income earners, increased expectations to work longer hours with less job security, rising costs of post-secondary education, technological developments that can overwhelm us, growing dependence on volunteerism to fill the gaps, and the perception of rising crime.

Each one of these trends can vary in personal importance to each of us, but each has the ability to complicate life by making any one area of life dominate to the exclusion of others. For example, if we feel pressure to work late every night and return a few work-related e-mails after we get home, work can become one of our roles that dominates to the point where other roles suffer. These other roles such as partner, parent, and so on may be put off, carried out in a half-hearted manner, or carried out well until we eventually run ourselves into the ground.

The opportunity for seamless living and the challenges to it posed by various trends underscore the difficulty we have in trying to figure out whether we have more or less leisure in our lives than we had in previous times. The only logical conclusion we can arrive at is that the comparison over time of leisure *time* is not meaningful, as it has very little if anything to do with true leisure. The best way to determine your leisure position is to ask yourself how you rate in terms of the three leisure criteria presented.

1. *Stress*. Do I experience more or less stress now than in the past?

2. *Living in the moment.* Am I satisfied with my ability to live in the moment or does living in the moment seem like a waste of time?

3. *Self-expression.* Do I have an inherent understanding of my most desired self-image? Am I satisfied with my ability to pursue experiences that bring me closer to that self-image?

However, we cannot proceed without at least some level of closure on the question of whether we have more or less leisure in a collective sense. There is no doubt that we thrive on the more creative elements of leisure, such as seeking out opportunities for self-expression. The range and depth of opportunities in our present age continue to multiply each day and we can thank technology for taking the lead role in that. There is also no doubt that today's workplace is increasingly sensitive to issues of balance. Education, though harder to access, has also evolved to become more flexible than ever before. As a population, we are in a better position today than in the past to find opportunities for self-expression and to achieve our full capacity.

On the other hand, it is hard to argue against the fact that we are more time-stressed and generally stressed than ever before. Unfortunately for us as a population, minimizing stress is the cornerstone of leisure—when we feel stressed, our ability to experience leisure as a moment of positive self-expression is hindered. What it often comes down to is the feeling we have when we've just rushed through a hectic mile-a-minute day to get to our child's Christmas concert and, although we sit through the entire performance, smiling and clapping at all the right places, our thoughts are racing through the three phone calls we forgot to make before we left, the two self-reminders about tomorrow's to-do list, a couple of problems that need mulling over, and the dilemma of what to make for supper when we finally get everyone home. The opportunity is there, but all too often we are not.

Where to from Here...

A look to the future is essential to maintaining our leisure ability. Just as a desired self-image is key to experiencing leisure in the first place, a forward glance to assess what external trends need to be negotiated in our future is also important. In the next two chapters we will focus on two key challenges to our future leisure ability. The first challenge is in dealing with a growing form of stress related to the shrinking pie phenomena, and the second is overcoming our predisposition to being productive such that we can discover our creative states.

• Chapter 12 •

Overcoming the Stress of the Shrinking Pie

We return to Rick, Lisa, Larry and Barb, whose employer has just merged with another company. They are mulling over the situation and their options one evening after work.

"The last few weeks have been quite the roller coaster around here, so what's keeping you so cool in all of this?" Larry asked Rick as they sat down at a table with Lisa.

"Oh, I think I've been just as stressed as anyone, but I know it's also not the end of the world," replied Rick.

Lisa looked up. "It's easier to stay cool if you're not staring at a mortgage and the prospect of paying big bucks for your kids' schooling down the road."

Larry said, "So Rick, what are you going to do around here?"

Rick, in a slow and measured manner, responded, "Susan and I decided last night that I should take the severance package and then we're going traveling for a year; there are just too many places I haven't been and too little time left to see them."

An astonished Larry said, "Are you crazy? How marketable are you going to be with a year missing from your résumé and all those kids just out of college so hungry for your job?"

"It really doesn't matter—I've put this off for years just because I've been so focused on work and I just can't pass this opportunity by. Susan and I have always seen ourselves as people who travel, except we've never really been able to let go and just travel," replied Rick.

"Well, Lisa, help me out here. Don't you think he's crazy?" asked Larry.

"Not that crazy. In fact, I think it's great," Lisa added with a smile.

"Oh no, Lisa, don't tell me you're taking your family to live off the land somewhere in the backwoods," groaned Larry, looking a little panic-stricken.

"No, we're staying here, but we might end up trading down for a smaller house while I...I"—all eyes are on Lisa—"go back to school," she blurted out.

"That's great, Lisa," said Rick. "What are you going to take up at school?"

"Don't laugh now, but I want to finish my graduate degree in psychology and get into private practice," Lisa explained.

"Do you know how much it's going to cost you to go back to school and how much you're going to lose in lost wages while you're setting up your own practice?" asked Larry.

"Yes, and it gets worse, Larry, because when I do set up my practice it's only going to be for two or three days a week," explained Lisa.

"You guys can't afford to live on that kind of money—" Larry began.

Lisa jumped in with conviction. "I told you, Larry, we've decided to downscale a bit for now and see how things work out. I'm tired of running at 100 percent just to survive and get through the day—life's just too fast, so I figure that I can spend more time with the kids and do something I've always wanted to do."

Rick said, "I think it's great—I've always seen you as the office psychologist anyway, so you might as well get paid for it."

Just then Barb joined them at the table. "Have a seat, Barb, and listen to this," Larry offered.

"You're no doubt talking about the changes," said Barb.

"Oh no, Barb, it's worse than that; Rick's taking the package and he and Susan are going to play world travelers for a year, and Lisa's going too except she's going back to school," Larry said, obviously expecting to find an ally in Barb.

"Well, I think that's great! I think a lot of people are deciding to go off in interesting directions," Barb replied.

Lisa asked, "So what are you going to do, Barb? I heard rumors you're staying."

"I heard you're getting a huge promotion. Well?" asked Larry.

"It's not official yet, but I think I'm staying on with the new company as the new VP of our area," Barb said, with hushed excitement. A collective "Wow!" sounded around the table.

"So this is what you want?" asked Rick.

"Oh yes, I can't tell you how much I want a shot at senior management. Ever since I finished high school I've worked for an opportunity like this, so I just had to jump at it when it came up," explained Barb.

"Barb, you know that your life is going to change in a big way now with all the travel involved and everything," warned Rick.

"I know and that part is a bit difficult, especially now, but I can change my arrangements with the kids and maybe rely on my mother a bit more. It's better in the long run for all of us. I've been bored these past two years, but now just think of the potential for impact and how maybe some of those ideas we've talked about can actually get off the ground!" Barb said with excitement.

"That's great, Barb, just don't forget me when you move into that corner office," pleaded Larry.

"Larry, I could not forget you if I tried. But tell me, what are you going to do?" responded Barb.

"I must be the only sensible one in this place, because my plan is to stay right where I am and fight for my job. I don't care if it means I have stay late every night and get up a 3 a.m. to send everyone e-mails, or if I have to walk the new boss's dog, because it's only a matter of time before the economy takes another hit, and when it does I'll be secure in my job. I'm digging in my heels around here," Larry said.

"I'm sure you'll do fine; everyone knows about what you've done here in the past," Lisa said reassuringly.

"I get the feeling that that's not so important any more—what I did in the past—and now I'll find myself elbow to elbow with all these young kids who can easily afford to have no life for the next five years," responded Larry.

"So what's the big deal? You can always find work, even if it's not here," said Rick.

"The big deal is that everything we have at home is based on my current wage—we're stretched. Since this whole buyout thing started I've been having nightly nightmares of Gail and me and the kids at the Salvation Army Christmas dinner, and we're not serving it either. This whole thing has made me so stressed," replied Larry, looking a little beaten.

"Do you think you're the only one around here that gets stressed? Look around, Larry, everyone is going through something like this," said Rick.

Lisa added, "Get a grip, Larry. I don't think these are the last changes by any means, so you'd better change your outlook or you're going to go crazy. You have choices, Larry. Whether you have stress or not is not one of your choices, but how you deal with it is, so you'd better decide what's really important, and where you want to be, and do something about getting there," said Lisa.

"Easy for you to say, Lisa; you and Rick are just opting out," replied Larry.

"There's nothing easy about the kind of decisions we've made, but at some level we know they're the right ones for us and that's all that matters," Lisa said.

Our characters experience the stress of everyday life much as all of us do. Each of our characters has struggled in dealing with their most recent challenge of change and uncertainty in the workplace which has clearly spilled over to the rest of their lives. Rick, Lisa and Barb have recognized opportunities within the situation because of their strong self-image. Rick has decided to slow life down and travel, knowing that his marketability may suffer a little but that he would suffer more if he didn't take the trip. Lisa has decided to make a major career and lifestyle change whereby she will end up with more time with her family, a job she loves, but less money and "stuff." Barb has decided to move up the corporate ladder because that is what she wants. In so doing Barb realizes she'll be putting in long work weeks but that very well may be her best form of self-expression—her leisure. These people have chosen to focus on the opportunity that often emerges from the rubble of stress and they'll likely be much happier for it.

On the other hand, Larry is focusing on the loss of the old ways with no powerful self-image to guide him through the challenge and into the future. The stress he is feeling will hinder the possibility of being open to leisure experiences. He has decided to work more but, unlike Barb, Larry will do so only because he feels he has to, and in that case work becomes an obstacle to leisure. There's little doubt that Larry's stress will spill over and affect his entire family as well.

No one is in a position to avoid stress but we are in a position to decide whether we will look for the opportunities within any challenge. In the next two chapters we will take the lessons learned from Rick, Lisa, Barb and Larry and explore ways to manage stress and find opportunities for self-expression in our changing world. In the final chapter we will bring these ideas together in the form of guiding principles that will help us rediscover leisure.

The Shrinking Pie

The stress we experience comes from countless different sources, some of which have a greater impact than others. In this chapter we will examine the phenomenon of "the shrinking pie" because of its growing relevance and explore ways to overcome this potential obstacle to our future leisure ability. Dealing with stress is essential to leisure because when we do so successfully we achieve the *freedom from* aspect of leisure.

The shrinking pie phenomenon is similar to a game of musical chairs. Every time the music stops in the birthday-decorated room, there is one less chair and one more child standing along the wall watching the others compete for the last chairs that remain. So goes the game of musical chairs. But the disappointment those kids experience is only temporary, because they know they'll get another chance. What if it were not a game, and standing along the wall meant missing out on something important? Many of the trends related to the widening of the gap between the haves and have-nots seem to result in a real-life game of musical chairs.

The widening of the gap is perhaps the greatest threat our future leisure ability faces both for the haves and the have-nots. The have-nots experience the debilitating stress of disadvantage in a world that is prospering. The haves are increasingly preoccupied with the stress of maintaining their position—their piece of the pie.

The shrinking pie is a metaphor for how we feel when the pool of available resources appears to be diminishing—resources that we need, want or simply expect to get, such as financial well-being, personal space, a healthy environment, good jobs, and even opportunities and hope. A friend of mine, in the midst of a messy corporate reorganization, described the mood of the workplace aptly: "It's like when the water level in the watering hole goes down and all the animals begin to look at each other a little differently." When the pool of available resources begins to shrink both the haves and have-nots begin to look at each other a little differently. The dangerous part of the widening of the gap is that many of us begin to take on a mentality of "I'm missing out on all this prosperity" or "I'm not getting what I deserve" or "I had better really hustle to keep my piece of the pie." These basic thought patterns, which are evident in many issues debated every day in the media, can bring about a preoccupation that seriously hinders leisure ability. The widening of the gap and the "pie is shrinking" mentality go hand in hand.

Show Me a Shrinking Pie

Some of us may be wondering what pie is actually shrinking, given the tremendous growth of the past decade. This mentality is most apparent during times of great disorder (like a war) or serious economic downturn, but there is strong evidence to suggest that it exists every day—even now. Not all the "pies" are strictly economic either; some have to do with our expectations of quality of life or the environment. In many cases, this mentality grows out of an incremental building of stress rather than an overnight impact (like a stock market crash).

The environment. The natural world is being developed faster than ever before and it provides perhaps the best example of the shrinking pie. People have organized themselves into groups to fight for each piece of pie. Developers tout economic prosperity and jobs (which are the bases for other pies) while environmentalists and outdoors enthusiasts argue prevention of environmental degradation and loss of future legacy. Developers retort that without continued growth, their piece of the pie will be lost to other global markets. Those who oppose developers believe that if they don't halt development, all will be lost and the entire pie will be gone forever. Regardless of the position, the result is a stress that eats away at our sense of freedom.

Personal space. North Americans expect a certain amount of personal space to move around in, allowing us to do what we want to do. Our world is getting crowded and congested; hence we have phenomena such as road rage or, at our ski areas, where skiers conflict with snowboarders, ski rage. Every day more groups are lobbying for restrictions on our pathways and parks to limit the use of mountain bikes or skateboards because they're thought to impede everyone else's enjoyment of these areas. Knowingly or unknowingly, right or wrong, those people who advocate restricted use are basically trying to reclaim their piece of the personal space pie.

Financial well-being. The size of the pie is somewhat confusing in this case because overall we are in the midst of strong economic growth, yet we still have a lower bracket whose piece of the pie is shrinking. At the same time we have those who are doing well but claim that their ability to expand their piece is being hindered by taxes and government restrictions. The shrinking pie of economic well-being is most apparent in developing countries. As one example, large tourism multinationals, often with the help of local governments, develop prime real estate and in some cases commodify local culture for profit. Locals seldom profit from this type of activity but it does leave them with a sense that their piece of the pie is shrinking. All too often, violence against those who are thought to be rich tourists or corporations can be rationalized by locals who feel their own options are being limited.

Government support. We've learned that the pie we call government support has shrunk. Nevertheless, it appears that everybody is lobbying in one way or another to get a piece of this pie or to keep their piece from getting any smaller. We want tax cuts, better health care, breaks for business, better education, school lunches, better roads, more policing and so on. We know government cannot do all these things but we still witness a vigorous struggle for each piece of this pie.

Education. The American Council on Education claims that a college or university education is becoming elitist because of rising costs. Tuition costs in Canada and the United States have typically risen faster than the cost of living, leaving many people standing along the wall in this real-life musical chairs game. The pie of available resources supporting education (a critical factor affecting leisure ability) is shrinking, causing stress for those struggling within the system and even more for those unable to attend.

Employment. As we enter the new millennium we find that jobs are plentiful—it is a pie that has actually increased. However, according to Jeremy Rifkin, the author of *The End of Work*, jobs will be a shrinking pie in the future due to worker displacement by technology. Rifkin made several controversial recommendations such as job-sharing and shorter work weeks as a way to better distribute jobs. His critics claim that job-sharing and shorter work weeks will never work, mostly because each of us would have to give up a little piece of our pie.

Technology. The only pie that seems to be truly growing is that of technology, with its blue sky of opportunity. However, I am inclined to believe that much of its growth is due to people who are desperately looking for a pie that is actually getting bigger instead of smaller. It's the only game of musical chairs on the block where, when the music stops, someone's mother actually adds a chair instead of taking one away. Excepting technology, the stress-inducing effects of the shrinking pie are incremental as they add a little to our stress levels each day.

Leisure Ability and the Shrinking Pie

The perception that we may be missing out on our fair share, that we are not getting what we think we deserve, or that we need to hustle if we're going to keep what we have are obviously stress-inducing—just as the dried-up watering hole that causes the animals to look at each other differently is stressful. But besides causing stress, this mentality may spring us into action to solve the problem (just as animals might find another hole, we might find a second job to make ends meet).

The stress we might feel as a result of the shrinking pie phenomenon can be compounded by a lack of confidence that any one pie will actually increase in the future. For example, those who believe that our wilderness areas are being eliminated experience stress not just at the loss of the space or the struggle to maintain it, but also because they do not believe that these areas (this pie) will get bigger in the future (so that everyone gets more). However, the shrinking pie phenomenon, with all its potential for stress, can also bring forth our bright, hopeful and innovative side.

Overcoming the Stress of the Shrinking Pie

Just as high spindly stratus clouds usually signal a change in the weather, the shrinking pie is a signal of change, and change is never completely bad or good—it is simply change. In essence, the shrinking pie phenomenon, as much as it is a source of stress, is also a catalyst for positive change. For example, in terms of the environment, the shrinking pie has forced many individuals and organizations to change their approach to the issue. Some environmental groups now direct their efforts to the purchase of wilderness lands to ensure their preservation—thus adding to the size of the pie. In the past 20 years we have begun to embrace low-impact camping techniques while in the wilderness to better protect the natural areas we have. In terms of overcrowding and quality personal space, we have witnessed a growing number of inner-city communities being reborn into diverse, livable and sustainable communities because they too once had to respond to a shrinking pie.

Stress usually comes before innovation. To only focus on the stress phase of the change is decidedly unhealthy and limiting to our leisure ability. At the same time we must recognize that such a phenomenon can bring about real and significant negative impacts. The key to overcoming the stress of the shrinking pie phenomenon is to recognize it as a cause for action—an alarm that should send us off in search of innovative solutions and new possibilities. Sometimes our only incentive to change is one less chair in the room.

Chapter References

American Council on Education. 1998. *Straight Talk About College Costs and Prices.* Report
of the National Commission on the Cost of Higher Education. January 21.

Rifkin, Jeremy, 1995. *The End of Work.* New York: G.P. Putnam's Sons.

• Chapter 13 •

Finding Creative Outlets

If we are to achieve our leisure potential now and in the future we must do more than manage our stress and live in the moment. We need to be able to find creative outlets for our self-expression. This is not so easy to do because we live in a world where most of us are largely predisposed to being productive rather than creative. However, it is those creative states (in a broad sense rather than simply taking up watercolors) that form the basis for much of the enjoyment and satisfaction we experience in our leisure.

To better understand our constant struggle to find creative states, consider the prominence of two types of actions in your everyday life: producing and creating. These two types of actions are not pure opposites by any means, but they do imply decidedly different approaches. The term *producing* conjures up thoughts of something quantitative, repetitive, obligatory and hurried, much like the activity of an assembly line worker. *Creating* makes us think about something more qualitative, expressive; something we desire and are immersed in, much like the work of an artist. If these two approaches, productivity and creativity, occupy two opposite ends of a continuum, which are you most oriented toward? Which of the two approaches sets the course for your day, and which of the two do you use to assess your accomplishments at the end of the day?

The answer to this question is an important gauge of how open we are to the leisure experience in everyday life, because states of creativity are those that have a greater affinity with the leisure experience.

It's an Uphill Struggle

Daily pressures and unavoidable obligations sometimes make us believe that finding opportunities for creativity and self-expression in our day is an uphill struggle. Whether we like it or not, most of us are more predisposed to being productive than to being creative. This is not surprising, since producing and economic production have long been associated with the success of North America and that type of historical philosophy stays with us a long time.

However, as we direct most everyday energies to being productive, we relegate creativity to something we do when there is time—free time. Whenever we are time-crunched, the creative side takes a back seat to the productive. This is not to say that leisure is impossible when we're focused on producing. In fact, productive energy can clear away stress-inducing tasks or simply create experiences that support our self-image. Some days we can get a great deal of satisfaction from clearing away all the items on our to-do list. However, we are less likely to find leisure in productive, task-oriented states than we are in creative, expressive states.

More importantly, a predisposition to productivity over creativity is as much a leisure constraint as any we have discussed, though less obvious than most. This constraint on our leisure ability can appear in the form of everyday pressures that force us to always look for the fastest route from point A to point B, where the end is always more important than the means. It is the kind of mentality that forces us to speed home from work for no other reason than to minimize the travel time instead of simply enjoying that time on the subway, on the bus or in the car. This is the kind of old-school mentality that is found in the economic model of leisure that states that leisure is the time remaining after one's work and maintenance obligations are met.

Competing Messages

The time-saving technology of the past 50 years was supposed to usher in free time, perhaps to be more creative—but instead it has been diverted to increase our productivity. We took efficiencies in washing clothes to mean that we should be washing them more often rather than redirecting those efficiencies to creative endeavors. Personal computers are more powerful than ever, so we can shave off seconds of waiting time and run more applications at once. Why create a letter from scratch when you can produce one using one of the many templates on your computer? In North America, we equate being productive (that is, doing more) with being smart.

Our basic predisposition to producing may explain why so many of the university students I teach appear to be singularly focused on the end goal of grades. Some of them grill me on my expectations for an "A" for each assignment and appear disappointed when I explain that what they think is more important than what I want. The creative part of the exercise is sometimes viewed as a waste of time because it complicates the straightforward path from point A to point B.

This should not be surprising, since the value of productivity is communicated to children at an early age. Each Christmas parents return to the question "whatever happened to the simple creative toys?" because of the perception that children's toys today require little imagination, unlike the wooden building blocks of the past. Similarly, the quantity of presents under the tree appears to be more important than the thought that could go into a few truly meaningful gifts. In school, the growing emphasis on standardized testing also does little to inspire creativity, but it does convey the message that we are all expected to function at a certain level. Teachers are often so panic-stricken over the possibility of a poor showing that other parts of the curriculum are bypassed in preparation for the tests. In essence, children learn to figure out what really matters (that is, what is rewarded) and arguably this is a skill that they eventually bring into the workplace.

When a young new employee enters a workplace, it does not take her or him very long to figure out what matters and what does not, which actions win a bonus compared to which ones are said to be important but go unrewarded. Often the message comes through the performance appraisal, which is invariably based on productivity measures, while creativity is something you do on your own time to be more productive. A similar message is sent when it comes to promotions. Young people in entry-level positions quickly realize that they score points not by making brilliant decisions (at that level they seldom have the opportunity to make far-reaching decisions) but by doing as much work as possible—never turn down a project even if you already have too many. This message is reinforced within most corporate annual reports, which are based on productivity measures.

Our predisposition to producing can act as an obstacle to our leisure ability. Sometimes it may feel as if our entire world is based on an accounting system that only measures units of production both at work and at home. Sometimes the things that matter the most are the things that can't be counted. Maybe that is why we see a growing trend toward simpler living, toward choosing to pursue what is important rather than just the "stuff" that can be counted. Similarly, this is a question many young parents face when deciding whether to work more at a time when money is usually tight and job security low, or spend more time with the family.

Judging by most of the messages we get and send concerning producing and creating, one might conclude that if God *created* the world in six days, most everything since then has been *produced*. Finding opportunities for our creative states that support leisure certainly can be an uphill struggle. Why is this?

We Do What Others Reward Us For

Yes, this is a generalization and yes, we can still find rebels among us who keep us on our toes. But think about how this statement applies to your own life. What gets priority in your life, or in your day? What are the things that tend to bump other, less important things? Are you rewarded at work for having a balanced life or are you accommodated? When we first enter a new job we learn what matters most (what gets the rewards) and what matters less, and then most of us proceed to do what we get rewarded for, regardless of what we may think is important.

Some workplaces tend to reward "appearing busy" as much as they reward actual accomplishments. This can make many of us feel compelled to work late into evenings and weekends, bring work home, send e-mails to the boss at all hours of the night, and complain about it at the water cooler. If being in the office is something that is rewarded, it can make picking up a sick child from school a very stressful experience.

Many of the debates and issues we see played out in the media are all about different groups with different reward systems. We talk about breaking down silos in the workplace—for example, increasing cooperation among different departments—but until we are rewarded for doing so we are not likely to risk leaving the comfort of our silos. Doing what we are rewarded for guides much of what we do; finding creative states for leisure is difficult because we're seldom rewarded by others for finding those creative states.

What to Do? What to Do?

If our predisposition to productivity over creativity in the workplace makes finding creative and expressive states an uphill struggle, that is not the case when it comes to our non-work sphere. It appears that North Americans are inclined toward the philosophy "work hard and play hard." Over the past several decades, our opportunities for self-expression in the non-work part of our lives have exploded.

The competition for our leisure dollar has grown tremendously. Technological advances in the areas of entertainment, communication, travel, outdoors and learning have given us countless new ways to play and easier access to these opportunities. The recent resurgence of the corporate play culture in some pockets of the United States and Canada has given us everything from the casual Friday to the three-sport-a-day corporate go-getters (people who feel compelled to play at least three sports a day on their weekends). Are we so predisposed to being productive that we have it color the way we pursue typical leisure activity?

Creating Creative States

For those of us concerned with expanding or even maintaining our potential for leisure as a moment of positive self-expression, it may be important to counter our natural predisposition to productivity with conscious creative opportunities. Think of the producing and creating dichotomy as two ends of a circular dial, much like an old-style volume dial. Sometimes you may need to purposefully walk over and tweak the dial yourself, because it's not going to change on its own.

We need to recognize our natural predisposition toward producing rather than creating as an important leisure constraint to negotiate around. Some people find it difficult to even attempt to balance these within a fast-paced environment, so they opt for a simpler job and simpler life. That is not always possible (or even desirable), so some people rely on their non-work periods to satisfy their need for creativity. However, our free time is becoming more scarce as the pace of our daily lives quickens, and even if we find some free time there is no guarantee that what we do in it will bring about a leisure experience. Another option, and one that is growing in popularity, is to do and be what we want to do and be—to live seamlessly.

The key is to do what you enjoy and receive satisfaction from doing it, and thus position yourself in a life of creative self-expression. If it's true that we do what we are rewarded for, then there may be nothing better than being rewarded for doing what you love to do.

• Chapter 14 •

Winning the Human Race

O ver the years I have had the pleasure of meeting up with past workshop participants and students, and the best part of seeing them is when they tell me that the experience we shared has changed the way they think of leisure. As far as I can determine we're not talking about monumental change, nor has anyone gone off to join a commune, but some small part of his or her life has changed for the better. Each one, and each in an individual way, has rediscovered leisure in their lives, first by being open to the idea that leisure is actually much more than free time and then by realizing the possibilities it can bring. In essence, they have freed themselves from the nailing-Jello-to-the-wall idea of chasing leisure as free time and have begun to think of leisure as an approach to life—as *a course of life we can choose.*

This book is intended to bring forth the realization that leisure is not only much bigger than free time, but we achieve leisure as a moment of positive self-expression when we know what we want and are prepared to negotiate all of life's challenges to get it. *It's Not About Time!* may help bring out your long-awaited reunion with leisure, perhaps like an unexpected reunion with an old friend who, you suddenly discover, has lived in the same city as you for the past 20 years. However, rediscovery is only the beginning because even a reunion can be awkward if you're not sure how to proceed with each other. Now we must organize our thinking toward action.

Winning the Human Race

The one who wins the human race is not the fastest, or the one who can multi-task the best, or even the one with the most money or stuff. The winner of the human race is the one who can set her or his own course based on their self-image—this is the key. This is sometimes easier said than done. Setting your own course in our pressure-filled and fast-paced world can be like playing a video car-race game where it's almost impossible to move at the speed you want without quickly crashing or sliding off the track. However, if we take the right approach, that is, that leisure is a lifelong pursuit, then a world of possibilities becomes attainable.

To set us on the right course we must briefly revisit some key lessons learned over the previous chapters.

1. **It's not about time.** Today most of us live in such a way that the different parts of life have blended and overlapped, making leisure as free time quite meaningless. Besides, if we look for leisure as free time we'll find that it's scarce and provides no guarantee of actually experiencing leisure.

2. **Leisure is the experience of living in a moment of positive self-expression.** It is a deeply personal experience whereby we experience in time an act that brings us closer to our self-image—to the person we believe we can be. Central to this idea is our ideal self-image that guides our everyday choices toward leisure experiences once it is clearly formed in our minds.

3. **We seek freedom to and freedom from.** Our search for leisure (our self-image) is guided by our basic desire to find the freedom to become the person we have the ability to become and the freedom from the stresses and oppression of everyday life. This means that, in order to find opportunities for our creative self-expression, we must find ways to manage and overcome stress.

4. **We negotiate leisure.** We don't live in a controlled laboratory setting, we live in a complicated world where external factors impact what we think, how we feel and how we act. Trends and developments in the world around us influence many aspects of our lives, including our ability to experience leisure. Some trends and developments provide us with greater leisure ability while others hinder leisure ability.

5. **Leisure is dynamic.** Our ideal self-image does not remain the same throughout our lives. It changes as we change. That means our leisure negotiation must take into account ever-changing external factors as well as our ever-evolving self-image.

Rediscovering Leisure in Our Changing World

There is no simple road map to rediscovering leisure. It is far too personal and dynamic to lend itself to a simple road map. However, there are 10 critical guiding principles that will allow you to set your own course toward rediscovering a meaningful, satisfying and enjoyable way to live. The guiding principles listed below are not set in any hierarchical order so you may find yourself skipping over some only to return to them later, which is not surprising given the dynamic nature of leisure. Only you know where to begin and only you know how well you are progressing on your journey of rediscovery.

Guiding Principles for Your Journey

1. What if I did nothing?

The best way to know just how ready you are to embark on a meaningful journey of rediscovery is to ask yourself, what if I did nothing? If you answer this question with the realization that doing nothing would mean failing to achieve your full potential in life, then you are a strong candidate for this journey.

For example, Rick and Lisa realized that doing nothing was not really an option in their lives because their present course did not match their respective self-images. So they embarked upon their own journeys of rediscovery. Larry has not come to this conclusion as of yet, so his future will continue to be colored by survival-driven stressful experiences.

2. What really drives you?

What is your ideal self-image? Is it clear in your mind? What do you currently do that supports this image in your own life? What are the obstacles preventing you from achieving a lifestyle filled with self-image-supporting experiences? Achieving a clear self-image is all-important to achieving leisure in your life.

In the narrative, Barb possessed a strong and clear self-image of herself as a successful manager and mother. It is an image that she pursued throughout her adult life and one, no doubt, that involved difficult negotiations.

3. Sometimes we have to break from the pack

We constantly receive (and send) messages that tell us to be and act like everyone else, and this can be stifling to our leisure ability. Peer pressure messages that tell us to be efficient at the cost of being creative, to focus on making as much money as possible now before the next down-cycle in the economy, to abandon everything you know for the latest shift whether it's the Internet or globalization (or the next one), to be distrustful and suspicious of others and more. These messages drive us to stay in a pack that may feel safe but that can also be restrictive.

Staying in the pack can be comfortable some days but we cannot forget that leisure is an individually experienced phenomenon, so breaking out of the pack to be our own person can be an important step toward rediscovering our sense of leisure.

For example, Rick and Lisa felt the pressures to stay in the pack, as most of us do, yet they chose to step out of the pack in their own way. Rick chose to travel while in mid-career and Lisa opted to downscale her material world in return for a more satisfying lifestyle overall. Rick and Lisa made conscious decisions about how willing they were to submit to life's symbols of success and in so doing they began creating their own symbols of success.

4. Look for creative outlets

That is not to suggest you go off to become an artist, but rather to look for creative outlets in your everyday life. It may simply be the approach you take to your day and whether you choose to take the most direct route from A to B or the one that is most satisfying and meaningful. The ideal creative outlet is a lifestyle built upon activity that is supportive of and in harmony with your self-image—a lifestyle where you do what you love. This may appear unrealistic, but when we think of leisure as a journey rather than an activity anything is possible.

Lisa decided to change careers—even knowing the short-term hardships—so that she can do what she wants and live the way she wants. Certainly challenges will present themselves to her in her new direction as in the past, but they may be just a little easier to deal with, knowing that every day has the potential to be an act of self-expression.

5. Pace yourself

Sure, life can be too fast but it can also be too slow for some of us. The pace of life can seriously affect our ability to experience leisure by affecting our ability to live in the moment. Some of us who feel overwhelmed by the fast pace of life may need to readjust priorities to slow it down—much like Rick in the narrative. Others may feel the need to speed it up, like Barb. The key is not the pace of life, but choosing a pace that is right for you. Boredom is as much a distraction as a sense of being overwhelmed—you need to find a pace that allows you to live in the moment.

6. Learn to understand your stress

Earlier in the book I gave a definition of stress as being a mismatching of one's expectations with what's actually happening (when the world does not unfold as it should). That was my attempt to better understand my stress and ultimately to figure out how to better manage my stress such that it does not impede my ability to live in the moment. Think about your stress—what brings it on? What reaction does it bring out in you and how does that reaction affect the people around you? How do you respond to stress when you finally realize that you're locked in its grip? Understand your stress so that you can recognize its onset and better manage it along the way. Stress kills leisure by preventing us from being there to live in the moment so it is worth the effort to better understand it. If Larry understood his stress in the first narrative he might have been able to salvage part of his disastrous ski weekend with his family.

7. Pick a moment and be there

Living in the moment is essential to achieving leisure but for many of us it is not an ability that comes to us naturally—sometimes we have to work at it. Pick a moment and be there—soak up all that the moment has to offer, whether you are on top of a mountain (where focusing on the moment is a little easier) or in the middle of a chaos-filled home getting supper ready (where it is not so easy to focus on the moment). Try to eliminate all distractions and simply focus on the one thing that you are doing and not on all the other things that may need to get done. You may be surprised at how enjoyable doing one thing can be.

8. Be aware of the trends around you

Achieving leisure is a constant negotiation between your internal drive and your external environment. You need to be aware of trends and developments that impact you now or may impact you in the future. Some trends may create a window of opportunity that will propel you on your journey of rediscovery while others may only present obstacles and challenges. Regardless, these external factors represent a big part of the everyday negotiation we undertake.

All four characters in our narrative were in constant negotiation with external factors such as economic cycles, volunteer pressures, workplace changes, globalization and others. Those who were more successful in achieving leisure were the ones who realized that opportunities are more likely to be found if we're looking for them.

9. Don't give up

There is no point at which we have arrived at our full leisure potential, so don't give up when on the journey you encounter a small setback. Similarly, make sure you celebrate your successes along the journey, however large or small. Most setbacks we will encounter are learning opportunities that will tell us a little bit more about who we are and what we are looking for.

We may experience setbacks because our ideal self-image is not quite clear enough, or if we underestimate the power of external factors. Rick, Lisa and Barb likely experienced many setbacks before they were able to align their internal and external factors to make their great leap forward. There is always hope, even for Larry.

10. Have fun

It's not supposed to feel like work.

Parting Thought...

It is not so much that we are afraid of change, or so in love with the old ways, but it is that place in between we fear...it is like being between trapezes. It is Linus when the blanket is in the dryer.
Marilyn Ferguson, *The Aquarian Conspiracy*

If there is one thing I have learned about the pursuit of real leisure, it is that it's not always easy for a variety of reasons, whether it is the fear of making the leap from what we know (even if we are not happy with it) to what we don't know, or being unsure of what we want, or the paralysis of stress. What I do know is that nothing sets the heart into motion like the idea of the freedom to become the person we can be. If there is a compass point to lead us to the start of the rediscovery period, it must be the possibility of being this person because we can. And each day we bring ourselves one step closer to our ideal self-image, we gain more strength to deal with life's stresses and tribulations. Stress will never go away, but what makes it surmountable is our desire and belief that we will negotiate it and still achieve our full capacity.

Chapter References

Ferguson, Marilyn. 1987. *The Aquarian Conspiracy*. Los Angeles: St. Martin's Press / J.P. Tarcher.

Harris, Jim. 1998. *The Learning Paradox: Gaining Success and Security in a World of Change*. Toronto: Macmillan Canada.

Related Reading

Academy of Leisure Sciences. White Paper #8: *The Problem of Free Time: It's Not What You Think.* http://www.eas.ualberta.ca/elj/als/alswp8.html

Adams, Michael. 1998. *Sex in the Snow: Canadian Social Values at the End of the Millennium.* Toronto: Penguin Books.

Beck, Nuala. 1993. *Shifting Gears: Thriving in the New Economy.* Toronto: Harper Collins Publishers Ltd.

Best, Patricia. 1999. "Play for Fun – and Profit!" *Report on Business.* August.

Csikszentmihalyi, Mihaly. 1997. *Finding Flow: The Psychology of Engagement in Everyday Life.* New York: Basic Books.

Dertouzos, Michael. 1997. *What Will Be: How the New World of Information Will Change Our Lives.* New York: HarperEdge.

Edginton, Christopher R.; Jordan, Debra J.; DeGraaf, Donald G.; and Edginton, Susan R. 1995. *Leisure and Life Satisfaction.* Dubuque IA: Brown & Benchmark Publishers.

Farina, John. 1991. "Perceptions of Time." In *Recreation and Leisure: Issues in an Era of Change.* State College, PA: Venture Publishing Inc.

Ferguson, Marilyn 1987. *The Aquarian Conspiracy.* Los Angeles: St. Martin's Press / J.P. Tarcher.

Figler, K. Stephen, and Whitaker, Gail. 1995. *Sport and Play in American Life.* Dubuque, IA: Brown & Benchmark Publishers.

Foot, David K., and Stoffman, Daniel. 1996. *Boom Bust and Echo: How to Profit From the Coming Demographic Shift.* Toronto: Macfarlane Walter & Ross.

Frederick, Judith. 1993. "Are You Time Crunched?" *Canadian Social Trends*. Statistics Canada, Winter.

Galbraith, John Kenneth. 1996. *The Good Society*. New York: Houghton Mifflin Company.

Goodale, Thomas L. 1991. "If Leisure Is to Matter." In *Recreation and Leisure: Issues in an Era of Change*. State College, PA: Venture Publishing Inc.

Homeschool.com. "Frequently Asked Questions about Homeschooling." www.homeschool.com

Kelly, John R. 1987. *Freedom to Be*. New York: Macmillan Publishing Company.

Maclean's /CTV Poll. 1995. "*Maclean's*/CTV Year-end Poll." *Maclean's* Magazine.

Maclean's/CTV Poll. 1999. "*Maclean's*/CTV Year-end Poll." *Maclean's* Magazine.

Neulinger, John. 1991. "Economics and Leisure, a Multifaceted Relationship: Toward More Free Time or a Freer Person?" *Journal of Leisure and Recreation*. World Leisure and Recreation Association, Spring.

Popcorn, Faith. 1991. *The Popcorn Report*. New York: Doubleday.

Rechtschaffen, Stephan. 1996. *Time Shifting: Creating More Time to Enjoy Your Life*. New York: Doubleday.

Reid, Angus. 1996. *Shakedown: How the New Economy Is Changing Our Lives*. Toronto: Doubleday Canada Limited.

Rifkin, Jeremy, 1995. *The End of Work*. New York: G.P. Putnam's Sons.

Robbins, Anthony. 1986. *Unlimited Power*. New York: Fawcett Columbine.

Saul, John Ralston. 1997. *Reflections of a Siamese Twin: Canada at the End of the Twentieth Century*. New York: Viking.

Spry, Irene M. 1991. "The Prospects for Leisure in a Conserver Society." In *Recreation and Leisure: Issues in an Era of Change*. State College, PA: Venture Publishing Inc.

Stebbins, Robert, A. 1997. "Casual Leisure: A Conceptual Statement." *Leisure Studies*. Vol. 16.

Weber, Max. 1922. *Economy and Society*. Berkeley: University of California Press.

Related Reading

Wolf, Michael J. 1999. *The Entertainment Economy: How Mega-Forces Are Transforming Our Lives*. New York: Times Books.

Zuzanek, Jiri; Beckers, Theo: and Peters, Pascale. 1998. "The 'Harried Leisure Class' and Canadian Trends in the Time from the 1970s to the 1990s." *Leisure Studies*. Vol. 17.

About the Author

Joe Pavelka began his work in the field of leisure as a camp counselor in Hamilton, Ontario, later obtaining degrees in Geography and Outdoor Recreation from Lakehead University, and a master's degree in Recreation Administration from the University of Alberta. Since 1990, Joe has worked in market research, community development and planning with Calgary Parks and Recreation. He also owns and operates Planvision Management Consulting Ltd., which focuses on leisure, recreation and tourism projects.

Joe is currently working as a full-time instructor of Eco-tourism and Outdoor Leadership at Mount Royal College and as a part-time instructor in the Leisure, Tourism and Society program at the University of Calgary. He has published a variety of articles and speaks at numerous conferences.

Joe can be reached directly at Planvision@home.com

Creative Bound Resources
A division of Creative Bound Inc.
Books that inspire, help and heal
www.creativebound.com

Supporting the business community
with lifestyle resources for personal growth
and enhanced performance.

Creative Bound authors are experts in a variety of lifestyle areas, including: stress control and life balance, leisure strategies, motivation, mental training (in sports, work and life), goal setting, enhancement of personal and professional performance, healthy relationships—both intimate and professional—and parenting and family management.

Joe Pavelka is a proven workshop facilitator and keynote speaker. He is available to speak on a variety of topics relating to *It's Not About Time! Rediscovering Leisure in a Changing World*. Workshops and keynote presentations are tailored to the needs of each group for optimal impact.

Please contact **Creative Bound Resources** at 1-800-287-8610,
by e-mail resources@creativebound.com or
visit our Web site at www.creativebound.com for more information.

We hope you have enjoyed
It's Not About Time!
Rediscovering Leisure in a Changing World

To order additional copies of *It's Not About Time!* by Joe Pavelka, please contact Creative Bound Inc. at 1-800-287-8610 (toll-free, North America) or (613) 831-3641. Associations, institutions, businesses and retailers—ask about our wholesale discounts for bulk orders.

ISBN 0-921165-69-2 $21.95 CAN
184 pages $17.95 US

Books that inspire, help and heal

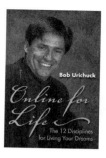

Online for Life:
The 12 Disciplines for Living Your Dreams

Do you know who you are?
Do you love what you're doing?
Do you have what you want out of life?
Do you *know* what you want out of life?
Are you "committed" to anything?
Are you thankful for each new day?

If you answered "no" to any of these questions, but want to say YES! to all of them, this book will inspire you to take control of your life. Bob Urichuck's acclaimed 12 Disciplines will provide you with a step-by-step, *inside-out* approach to finding the authentic you. With discipline, direction, and new tools in hand, you'll soon be living the life of your dreams!

Internationally respected speaker and trainer **Bob Urichuck** helps individuals and organizations identify their objectives and the disciplines needed to achieve them. The results are measurable and lasting.

ISBN 0-921165-65-X $19.95 CAN
200 pages $15.95 US

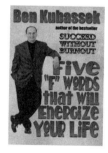

Five "F" Words That Will Energize Your Life
Simple steps to move your life from Burnout to Balance

In response to the success of his bestseller *Succeed Without Burnout*, entrepreneur, author and professional speaker **Ben Kubassek** explores the five "F"s of Fitness, Family, Friends, Finances and Faith, and takes a deeper look at these essential ingredients of a happy, fulfilled and balanced life.

ISBN 0-921165-61-7 $16.95 CAN
184 pages $12.95 US

Books that inspire, help and heal

Vitamin C for Couples
7 "C"s for a Healthy Relationship

The Prescription:
- Caring
- Change
- Communication
- Connection
- Conflict
- Creativity
- Commitment

Practicing the 7 "C"s described in this book will help to make a good relationship even better. Just as you take Vitamin C to build up your immune system and keep your body healthy, a regular dose of the 7 "C"s will bring you closer to your partner and keep your loving relationship strong.

Luke De Sadeleer, the Couples Coach™ is a professional speaker, author and facilitator, encouraging people to take control of their lives and recover their passion.

ISBN 0-921165-65-X $18.95 CAN
216 pages $15.95 US

Laughter, Love & Limits
Parenting for Life

With warmth, wisdom and wit, **Dr. Maggie Mamen** (author of *Who's in Charge: A Guide to Family Management*) explores the various myths associated with parenting, and creates a general parenting philosophy with three main goals:

- #3 Loving children enough to set reasonable limits until they can set limits of their own;
- #2 Giving ourselves, as parents, permission to be leaders in the family;
- #1 Showing our children that there is hope for the future.

The result is an approach that is useful for children of any age, from the cradle, through the teen years and beyond. *Laughter, Love & Limits* provides support and reassurance in the most important job anyone can ever undertake: Parenting for Life!

ISBN 0-921165-54-4 $18.95 CAN
208 pages $15.95 US

Call to order: **1-800-287-8610** *(toll-free in North America)*
or write to: Creative Bound Inc., Box 424, Carp, Ontario, Canada K0A 1L0

www.creativebound.com